THE PASSIONATE LIVES & LEADERS SERIES

James R. Lucas & Phil Hotsenpiller

THE ATTRACTION PRINCIPLE:
FINDING, KEEPING, AND
TEAMING PASSIONATE PEOPLE

Quintessential Books

READ BOLDLY. THINK DEEPLY. LIVE PASSIONATELY.
www.quintessentialbooks.com
BOSTON • KANSAS CITY

Copyright © 2009, Quintessential Books.

This Book Is Copyrighted Material. All Rights Are Reserved. It Is Against The Law To Make Copies Of This Material Without Getting Specific Written Permission In Advance From Quintessential Books. No Part Of This Publication May Be Reproduced, Stored In A Retrieval System, Or Transmitted In Any Form Or By Any Means, Electronic, Mechanical, Photocopying, Recording, Or Otherwise, Without Prior Written Permission Of The Publisher.

International Rights And Foreign Translation Rights Are Available Only Through Negotiation With Quintessential Books.

Printed In The United States Of America
ISBN 978-0-9823161-1-5

Cover & Layout Design by Barberhaus Design Studios
Cover Design by Jonas Barber
Layout Design by JV Kennedy

Author Photo Of James R. Lucas Copyright © 2006
By Decloud Studio. All Rights Are Reserved. Used By Permission.

Author Photo Of Phil Hotsenpiller Copyright © 2008
By Barry Morgenstein Studios. All Rights Are Reserved. Used By Permission.

READ BOLDLY. THINK DEEPLY. LIVE PASSIONATELY.

Visit Quintessential Books At www.quintessentialbooks.com
For More About Passionate Lives And Leaders, Visit www.livesandleaders.com

All Trademarked Terms Are The Property Of Luman International, Inc. All Rights Are Reserved.

TABLE OF CONTENTS

Introduction: The Attractive Power of Passion 6

Part 1: Identifying People of Passion 18

Part 2: Matching People Who Share Your Team's Passion 40

Part 3: Keeping and Developing Passionate People 50

    10 Keys to Keeping & Developing Passionate People™ 52

Part 4: Teaming People of Passion 62

    7 Keys to Effective Teams™ 66

Time for Action 71

THE ATTRACTIVE POWER OF PASSION

Great people—people who are passionate about what you do and about their own contribution, and who have the ability to add value—have always been hard to find and keep. They have the most options, they're the most in demand, and they know it. They are first rate and don't have to accept a second-rate situation.

On the other hand, isn't it really easy to find inadequate people? And once you've got them, isn't it hard to get rid of them? Non-contributors—people who are negative about what you do and hate their jobs and who have the ability to destroy value—have always been easy to find and hard to eliminate. They have few options (or none), they're not in demand anywhere, and they often know it. They are second-rate and aren't going to give up a second-rate situation.

> **DO YOU FEEL LIKE IT'S REALLY HARD TO FIND GREAT PEOPLE? AND AFTER YOU FIND THEM, TO KEEP THEM?**

Have you ever fired anybody too soon? We've asked thousands of leaders this question, and no one has ever said "yes." Most of them have said, "I've taken way too long with way too many people." In this book, we're going to talk very clearly about how to avoid facing the firing decision very often—by making solid hiring decisions and building a passionate team.

If we don't become experts at hiring, we're going to have to become experts at firing. This is a much less effective core competency than getting it right from the start. There are better things to focus on than HR policies and disciplinary processes and the legal aspects of terminating staff.

Hiring excellence means asking new and vital questions. How do we find and then keep
- truly passionate, committed, performance-oriented people?
- people who want to have a real stake in our success?
- people who are going to take our organization to the next level?
- people who will allow us to meet or exceed the expectations of all of our stakeholders?

Finding these people is not just a matter of spending more time on interviewing and hiring, which is what many people have recommended. You can spend a lot of time and still end up with a terrible hire. Most of the recruiting and hiring practices we've seen have little chance of finding "believers and winners." It's a matter of spending the time on the things that are going to make a difference.

THE ATTRACTION PRINCIPLE

If we're going to find and keep passionate people, it starts with attracting them—with getting them to participate in our hiring process in the first place. We have to let them know that we exist and that we're worth considering. We want the magnetic core of our organization's passion to turn the needle of their compasses our way.

What key aspects of an organization allow you to attract these difference-makers? Or, to say it differently, *what can you do to make your organization attractive?* Here are five important "Attractions":

FIVE ATTRACTIONS FOR PASSIONATE PEOPLE:
Have a larger-than-life vision
Talk about passion
Differentiate
Offer the 10 Keys
Think and talk multi-generationally

Attraction 1: Have a larger-than-life vision.

FIVE ATTRACTIONS FOR PASSIONATE PEOPLE:
> HAVE A LARGER-THAN-LIFE VISION
   Talk about passion
   Differentiate
   Offer the 10 Keys
   Think and talk multi-generationally

Right off the bat, you want to separate the people who are looking for a *job* from those who are looking for a *life*.

The only starting point for drawing a higher proportion of passionate people is to offer something *no one else ha*s – a unique, stirring vision. Everyone can offer money and benefits and hygiene factors (like nice facilities and amenities), and some can probably offer a lot more of those things than you can. If you focus on these peripherals, you're competing on everyone else's terms and can lose to the next bidder.

But no one else can offer your vision of the future and its possibilities. Most don't offer an attractive vision of *any* kind. You can get people seeing and dreaming things that deeply resonate with them, and imagining how they can fit in. You can go beyond *benchmarking* competitors' hiring practices to *benchbreaking* them. (For more on the importance of vision and how to establish one, see ***The Passion Principle: Designing a Passionate Organization***, the first title in the Passionate Lives & Leaders series).

A Contagious Passion

"I was frustrated before I actually became passionate about a vision," says Howard Dayton, founder of Crown Financial Ministries*, an organization dedicated to equipping people around the world to learn, apply, and teach solid financial principles. *"Up to that point, my total focus in life was getting rich. I didn't care about people, and money was my god."*

That all changed when Dayton encountered a set of compelling, timeless principles that put his fascination with wealth into perspective. *"When I saw what the Bible said about money, my entire life turned upside down,"* he recalls. He pauses to correct himself: *"Right side up, I should say."*

That moment of personal spiritual crisis became the source of a powerful vision. *"I became completely passionate about people learning what God said about money,"* says Dayton.

That vision has only grown. Crown has now taught or prepared more than 50 million people in over 40 nations. The organization relies on approximately 250 employees and over 10,000 passionate volunteers worldwide.

"From a leader's perspective, having a clear vision, having a God-given passion about which you're relentless, motivates you to be faithful over a long period of time" Dayton observes. *"As those around you catch the vision, the critical mass becomes larger and larger. When a person comes into your sphere who's interested in serving with you or being involved with you, the sphere just grows. More and more people have the vision; more and more people catch the passion."*

For Dayton, this process of multiplying a worthy vision isn't just a theory. He's seen it produce results in his organization and in the lives of people the organization trains. Several decades after Dayton's epiphany, that *"contagious passion"* remains the secret to the organization's growth and capacity to attract volunteers around the world.

This first Attraction is powerful with everyone, but even more so with dynamic younger people, who are much less concerned with "loyalty" and "security" and much more interested in meaning and purpose.

A larger-than-life vision will make the difference for your organization in many ways. One of the most significant is in what it can do for your recruitment.

---

*For more information on this organization, please visit www.crown.org

AN IRRESISTIBLE VISION

Summarize your current (or yet-to-be-developed) vision in a killer tag line:

_____

_____

_____

_____

Attraction 2: Talk about passion.

FIVE ATTRACTIONS FOR PASSIONATE PEOPLE:
Have a larger-than-life vision
> **TALK ABOUT PASSION**
Differentiate
Offer the 10 Keys
Think and talk multi-generationally

The funny thing about passionate people is that they love talking about passion. They're drawn to it and can't escape its pull. They're zealous about life and their place in it. They want to know if other people are passionate and what they're passionate about.

If we want to connect with potential hires, talking about passions (yours and theirs) is an outstanding place to start. If you talk about your passions and how your passions fit with your organization and they don't care, you just learned a lot and can say a gracious "goodbye." If they talk about their passions and those passions don't fit with your organization, you've also learned a lot and can wish them well–elsewhere.

INTERVIEWING FOR PASSION

Jot down 3 possible questions that you could ask to find out where a recruit's passions might be:

1._____

2._____

3._____

Luman International uses a 20-point Passion Scale™ and related questions with its clients to center hiring conversations on passion. We've learned not to be surprised that many organizations don't address *any* of these 20 passion deal-breakers.

If you don't start by talking about passion, it might be very hard to inject it later.

Attraction 3: Differentiate.

FIVE ATTRACTIONS FOR PASSIONATE PEOPLE:
Have a larger-than-life vision
Talk about passion
> DIFFERENTIATE
Offer the 10 Keys
Think and talk multi-generationally

Whether you're choosing between toothpastes, restaurants, or organizations, the hardest choices are often between options whose differences are small. We make it hard for people to choose us when we look just like every other pair of shoes on the rack.

If they can't see anything special about us, they'll end up making their decisions based on small differences (like 5 percent in salary or slightly better health insurance) or on differences we can't control (like the commuting distance or facility design).

We have to give people big differences on important things so that those compensation and benefits and hygiene differences fade into the background. We have to find ways to differentiate ourselves and then to express those differences in interesting ways. If we use *Reverse Mentoring*™, for example, where younger or newer people are given the opportunity to mentor older or senior people, we have a way to change recruits' entire perspective on our organization - and their potential place in it - from day one.

Like other organizations, Luman International publishes "Contact Us" information. But on certain materials, Luman includes a differentiator, a surprising twist: We have a section called *"Don't contact us if. . . ."* We tell potential clients not to contact us if they want to make only painless change or solve big problems without effort. The interesting discovery we made: potential team members, even more so than potential clients, kept telling us how much they loved this, how much it made them want to find out more about us and to consider joining us. They wanted to work for a company that would tell the truth and that was willing to walk away from bad business, no matter how profitable.

DIFFERENTIATING

Take a moment to write down 3 ways in which your organization or team is different from any other of which you are aware:

1._____
2._____
3._____

Now what? Hand this out to every recruit!

Attraction 4: Offer the 10 keys.

> **FIVE ATTRACTIONS FOR PASSIONATE PEOPLE:**
> Have a larger-than-life vision
> Talk about passion
> Differentiate
> **> OFFER THE 10 KEYS**
> Think and talk multi-generationally

Everyone wants good pay and benefits. Nice working conditions. A friend at work. Good equipment or tools. Praise. Educational opportunities. A cafeteria.

A short commute. A lot of "employee satisfaction" studies are built around these types of factors.

But more important for attracting passionate people (and then keeping them—and keeping them fired up) is to offer them the *10 Keys to Keeping and Developing Passionate People*™ (discussed later in this book) right from the start. If you really do provide people with a sense of freedom (one of the 10 Keys), tell them that. Start in the advertisement: "Do you yearn for a sense of freedom in your work?" Then make freedom a point of discussion early in the interview process, preferably at the first session. If you have put some metrics on the 10 Keys, bringing those up in the conversation can make a huge positive impression.

CONSIDERING THE KEYS

Without looking ahead in the book, give a little thought to what you think is on the list of 10 Keys (other than Freedom), and pencil them in here:

- _____
- _____
- _____

Later you can compare your first thoughts above with the 10 Keys that we have vetted with thousands of leaders over many years.

Attraction 5: Think and talk multi-generationally.

FIVE ATTRACTIONS FOR PASSIONATE PEOPLE:
Have a larger-than-life vision
Talk about passion
Differentiate
Offer the 10 keys
> THINK AND TALK MULTI-GENERATIONALLY

Everyone shares a common humanity, but the generation in which we live shapes and colors our definition of it.

People from the Depression and Second World War era were understandably very passionate about security and loyalty (often defined as "staying your whole career") that would be rewarded. People from the next generation were passionate about expanding opportunity and the chance to live a comfortable middle-class life. Like their Baby Boom parents, members of Gen X wanted interesting work that contributed to society in ways that transcended the product or service their organization provided. Millennials are seeking flexibility in their work arrangements on an unprecedented scale.

You need a consistent message (the first 4 Attractions) that can be customized for each of the age groups with which you'll be dealing. Give it a try.

CRAFTING A MULTI-GENERATIONAL MESSAGE

What would you say to each of the following about why they should be passionate about your team or organization?

A recent college graduate: _____
_____
_____
_____

Someone in their 20s or 30s: _____
_____
_____
_____

Someone in their 40s or 50s: _____
_____
_____
_____

Someone in their 60s or older: _____
_____
_____
_____

"MUTUALLY PASSIONATE PEOPLE FIND EACH OTHER. PASSION BEGETS PASSION. THE FEW THAT SHARE THE SAME INTENSITY ARE THE ONES WITH WHOM MUTUALLY BENEFICIAL RELATIONSHIPS CAN BE FORGED." MATT WEST, DRUMMER

A Lightning Rod Attracts Electricity

"Employees or associates who demonstrate strength of character, integrity, and demonstrating ethical behavior in all situations are cornerstones of any organization," says Harold Taber, former Group President & COO of the Coca-Cola Bottling Company of Los Angeles and President & CEO of Hansen Beverage Company, where he still serves on the Board of Directors. "There was no doubt in the HR department about the type of associate we were looking for. Basically, I purposed to create a work environment that would bring these people to us, as I continued to believe that people are a companies greatest asset."

Taber decided to create that magnetic environment by practicing "servant leadership": putting people–customers and associates–ahead of the bottom line and trusting that they would take care of the bottom line. His plan to make the company attractive to "winners and believers" included making the associates' families a company priority. It also included communicating to people how valuable they were and giving them regular encouragement and affirmation. To stress the point that the associates at Hansens were vital to the company's success, Taber led the charge to offer all potential associates stock in the company.

The stakeholders (stockholders, customers, suppliers and company associates) turned out to be the greatest source of recruitment. Because they believed in the company, they recommended it to others.

"Great word-of-mouth endorsement gets people interested and brings people in," Taber observes.

When top-notch people came through the door, Taber relied on values alignment to determine whether they would fit well into the company.

"I believe the employee or potential employee's personal value system should match up with the company," says Taber, who now serves as the Director of the MBA Mentor Program of the Crowell School of Business at Biola University. "If they don't match up, the employee will be in an uneasy situation, not understanding why the company makes the decisions it does."

Once he found someone whose values lined up with the company's, Taber made sure they also had passion for the work they would do.

"If you don't have fire in your belly at 8 o'clock on Sunday night to come in to work the next day," he asserts, "you're in the wrong company."

Taber charged the associates with acting on that passion: "If your church or your Little League isn't using our products," he'd tell them, "you need to do something about it. You're not just an administrative support person, you're a salesperson. Everyone is equally important to moving this company forward."

Creating an attractive culture paid off exponentially. "Our productivity level increased a minimum of 5 percent every year," Taber reports. "At Hansens, this was achieved with the right people in the right positions with the right proucts. Hansen Beverage Company is currently doing over a billion dollars in revenues, and Fortune *has called it one of the fastest growing stocks of the last decade."*

"HOW WE GO OUT AND FIND AND CHOOSE PEOPLE: WE ABSOLUTELY KNOW WHAT THE ESSENCE OF A REAL, TRUE "HOLLARDITE" IS - IN OTHER WORDS, SOMEONE WHO REALLY UNDERSTANDS OUR VALUES AND WHO WE ARE....WE HAVE ACTUALLY ARTICULATED VERY CLEARLY WHAT IT IS TO BE A HOLLARDITE AND WHAT IT IS NOT TO BE A HOLLARDITE."

SHEILA SURGEY, HEAD OF BUSINESS DEVELOPMENT & BRAND, HOLLARD, SOUTH AFRICA

"LET POTENTIAL CANDIDATES KNOW THAT YOUR ORGANIZATION CELEBRATES PEOPLE WHO HAVE A PASSION FOR THE TYPE OF WORK THE COMPANY DOES; THAT THEY CAN EXPECT TO WORK WITH OTHER ENGAGED EMPLOYEES."

DEBORAH MCINTYRE, VICE PRESIDENT - CARD SERVICES, WELLS FARGO BANK

IDENTIFYING PEOPLE OF PASSION

Here's a truth that voids almost everything that's been written or spoken on employee motivation: We can't inject passion into someone through motivational tricks and schemes.

There's no way to manufacture or fabricate passion. It simply has to come from within. Our job as leaders is not to create passion out of thin air, but rather to find passion that already exists and then fuel it by creating an environment where passion can flourish. We can certainly build passion in an organization that was not made up of people who were passionate from the start (for more information, see ***The Passion Principle: Designing a Passionate Organization,*** the first title in the Passionate Lives & Leaders series). But we've given ourselves an additional challenge that we would do well to avoid if possible.

So this means that identifying people of passion has just moved to the front of our list of considerations if we want to build a culture of passion and excellence.

Here are five major sources of "clues" to consider as we attract, recruit, interview, hire, and orient new people or team members:

FIVE CLUES TO CONSIDER:
Character
Passions and goals
Past performance
Education, training, and credentials
Assessments and diagnostic tools

Most hiring processes look at these clues in some manner, particularly at education, training, and credentials, but often too superficially to identify people of true passion and excellence, the people who are going to help us build the future.[1] Let's consider more deeply the clues that can tell us we've found what we need—and the clues that should tell us to run for the hills.

> **"STRONG PEOPLE ALWAYS HAVE STRONG WEAKNESSES . . .[BUT] THERE IS ONE AREA WHERE WEAKNESS IN ITSELF IS OF IMPORTANCE AND RELEVANCE. [THE ABSENCE OF CHARACTER AND INTEGRITY] FAULTS EVERYTHING ELSE. HERE IS ONE AREA WHERE WEAKNESS IS AN ABSOLUTE DISQUALIFICATION."**
> **PETER DRUCKER, RENOWNED AUTHOR AND MANAGEMENT EXPERT[2]**

Clue 1: Character

> **FIVE CLUES TO CONSIDER:**
> **> CHARACTER**
>   Passions and goals
>   Past performance
>   Education, training, and credentials
>   Assessments and diagnostic tools

The Signs of Attraction

When looking for clues from character, we first have to get past the superficial assessments: Do I like the person? Does he seem like he's honest? Has she robbed any convenience stores in her past life? Looking for impressions about this basic kind of honesty is far too superficial and way too narrow an approach.

The great industrialist and philanthropist Andrew Carnegie attributed his success to three qualities: "Concentration is my motto – first honesty, then industry, then concentration."[3] Honesty means much more than just not stealing or cheating. It means we have integrity, wholeness, consistency—what Emerson called "centrality, the impossibility of being displaced."[4] It means that we know who we are and what we're about. We're comfortable in our own skin.

Do the people we interview know who they are and what they're about? Or are they too young, immature, non-reflective, or arrogant to even see themselves and what they need realistically? They need to confront the reality of whether the opportunities they're seeking fit who they are.

> **"BY CONSTANT SELF-DISCIPLINE AND SELF-CONTROL YOU CAN DEVELOP GREATNESS OF CHARACTER."**
> **GRENVILLE KLEISER, AUTHOR**[5]

They need evidence of *self-discipline*, not a record of waiting around for others to impose discipline on them or tell them what to think or do.

They need a record of *positive relationships* with others that they can talk about and substantiate. As they discuss those relationships, there should be signs of grace – toward themselves and toward others, including the people who ruffled their feathers along the way.

Character includes *persistence* and signs of growth during difficult challenges. We want people who freely recognize problems and persist in overcoming them, people who can show battle scars from their hard fights to bring about positive change. An ability to overcome problems reveals their experience level, their ability to innovate, and whether or not they have any personal courage. Are they going to stick with you when things get tough (as things always do)?

We want people who are seeking to *make a difference*, not just to make a living. They should have ample amounts of Carnegie's "industry" and "concentration" (or focus). There should be some things that make them mad, and finding out what those are will give us additional insight into their character. Do they only get angry about their personal frustrations? Or do they spend their indignation on bigger things?

They should have some *curiosity*, an interest in new ideas and challenges and a willingness to look at things from a fresh perspective. People can be 20 years old and very old–or 80 years old and very young. What matters is mindset and perspective. We're looking for people who add energy when they enter the room, not people who drain the room dry.

When we tell them about problems in our organization (and we should do that, because honesty sets the tone), we need to see what kinds of *fresh, unique perspectives* they offer, even given only a small amount of information. They need to bring new ways of thinking about problems to the table. Look for indications of creativity and innovation. A naïve or judgmental reaction to problems is a very clear sign of a potentially problematic character.

This person's demeanor should have at least a trace of lightness or *humor* instead of total grim seriousness. It can be very burdensome to work with someone who isn't willing or able to laugh. Of course, we want to monitor humor for appropriateness in content, application, and timing. But wittiness is essentially an intersection between social and intellectual intelligence and is not a small thing in most positions.

The Warning Signs

Character warning signs would include
- fuzzy or ambiguous answers
- answers unsupported by evidence
- uneasiness when discussing certain professional issues, indicating that this person is not being fully open and transparent.

If people are trying to protect themselves rather than exploring whether there's a true match, keep looking. After all, people who aren't open and transparent during the interview phase aren't likely to change once they're on board. Team members who won't openly discuss problems or challenges or concerns end up introducing a contagion into the organization that could easily spread to other people.

LOOKING FOR CLUES

Pick a person of character in your organization. Note a few observations of how they exhibit the character qualities discussed above.

Integrity _____

Self-discipline _____

Positive relationships _____

Persistence _____

Seeking to make a difference _____

Curiosity _____

Unique perspective _____

Humor _____

Clue 2: Passions & Goals

> **FIVE CLUES TO CONSIDER:**
> Character
> > **PASSIONS AND GOALS**
> Past performance
> Education, training, and credentials
> Assessments and diagnostic tools

The Signs of Attraction

The word "amateur" comes from a Latin root that means "to *love*." What do the people you're interviewing love? There should be something that they would do even if they weren't paid for it, something that would get them up in the morning even if they were sick.

Once people understand their passions, we can help them find the opportunities in our organization or team that will stir their souls.

Perhaps the most important clue in any part of the interviewing process is the story. People need to be able to give us a coherent narrative of the arc of their lives and how they arrived at where they are today. For example, "I spent all of my life working up to this point in a non-leadership position. Here's what I want to accomplish with what I've learned by observing, and here's how all of the pieces fit together to allow me to take this supervisory role you're offering." Or, "I had one set of passions in an early part of my career, and I pursued those to their conclusion. Then I developed a new set of passions, and I'm pursuing those while drawing on all the lessons I learned in the first set. Here are some examples of what I've learned from that 'first life' that will help me be effective here."

There may be a lot of different plot lines, but people need to be able to tell us stories that make sense. If they seem confused about their lives and what they've done and how they got here, they're not going to be less confused after we've hired them. We're not looking for the people who bounce around taking whatever job they can convince somebody to give them, because they're not very likely to be good at it. And they definitely won't have the passion.

After we've heard these stories, we can follow up with specific questions about how particular previous jobs fit into the narrative. This gets us out of the "tell me about this job" rut that seldom tells us much. We want to know how each job or assignment fulfilled a passion, taught a valuable skill, or perhaps revealed to them where their passion *wasn't*. For example, "I had to paint houses to pay for classes to get the education I needed to do what I love." Or, "This has been my passion all along, but I was young. No one in my family or my circle ever knew how to do it, so I had to figure it out on my own. I've made a lot of mistakes, but I feel like I'm getting closer. And this is where I want to be now." If pieces of their stories don't make sense, they aren't ready to join your team.

People's stories show whether they're reactive or proactive in pursuing specific interests. The stories don't have to be smooth, but they at least need to show people thinking about what they've done, where they've been, and where they want to go. And as they present all of those facets, keep the character clues in mind.

The Warning Signs

We have to be careful that we don't turn interviews into mutual marketing blitzes where we're trying to sell them on a company that's better than it really is, and they're trying to sell themselves for jobs they may not really be passionate to do. Only honesty and transparency on both sides of the table will allow this relationship to work. If you start sensing that you're involved in an advertising campaign, remember the old Roman slogan: "Let the buyer beware."

LOOKING FOR CLUES

Take a moment to think about your story. Try to write it down as a concise narrative here:

_____
_____
_____
_____
_____

Now take another moment to think about the story of your most passionate direct report or colleague. Try to write it down as a short, concise narrative here, with emphasis on how this story ties into their passion and goals:

_____
_____
_____
_____
_____
_____

The Integrating Power of Integrity

"The whole idea came to me so quickly that I felt that it was a gift from God," says Mike Vande Mortel, describing the invention whose prototype he's currently building. The founder and president of the philanthropic organization Palm Sunday, he's also an accomplished athlete and pathbreaking inventor who holds many U.S. patents for his work.

"This idea not only has economic potential, but it saves lives because it takes the place of manual work that is inherently dangerous and kills and hurts a lot of people every year."

Although Vande Mortel remains ambiguous about the exact nature of what he calls a "pioneer invention" while it's still in development, he's outspoken about the passion that drives him forward: "This invention is an economic engine for philanthropic work," he says. "I think it would be really rewarding to reach the end of my life and know that God delivered a lot of really neat stuff, and that I was able to use that stuff to help underprivileged people and create jobs for people."

When the latest idea came to him, Vande Mortel put his passion to work right away, founding Palm Sunday as an avenue for investing eventual profits from his invention in those goals. His vision pulls other talented people into the project like iron filings to a magnet.

"There are a lot of people who have come together to make this happen. It really only happens when I stay out of the way," he acknowledges.

Rather than trying to "sell" potential collaborators on the project, Vande Mortel just gives them a straightforward account of what motivates him. "I guess when you're honest, honest folks show up through a program of attraction, not promotion," he says. "Folks that are put off by the transparency go away. It's a cool natural vetting process. To date, I have had the great fortune of meeting and working with folks who are really accomplished."

Vande Mortel's own passion for making a difference is rooted in the most profound crisis of his life.

"My life was turned around by a very tangible experience," he recalls. *"I had a moment of clarity and was struck sober. I have remained sober for 17 years. At the last minute, I said, 'God, save me. I'll do whatever you want me to do.' My life changed dramatically. It still impacts what I do today. Palm Sunday is motivated by this experience."*

The qualities that are so attractive to his fellow visionaries—Vande Mortel's passion and transparency—still spring from that raw moment.

"I feel like I have lived two lives," he says. *"I lived the wrong one first, but I've been living the right one ever since."*

Clue 3: Past Performance

FIVE CLUES TO CONSIDER:
Character
Passions and goals
> PAST PERFORMANCE
Education, training, and credentials
Assessments and diagnostic tools

The Signs of Attraction

The third major clue is past performance. People need to have delivered actual, verifiable results.[6]

This is where the rubber meets the road with the stories they've told us. We're not only asking for references to verify that they've told us the details of their employment and other past adventures correctly. We're not only asking for recommendations, which frankly almost anyone can supply. More than references and recommendations, we're asking for *hard evidence of what happened* in the last organization (without violating any non-compete or confidentiality agreements) or situation, and for a believable explanation of what they did to contribute to those solid results.

Sometimes people claim that their prior organizations achieved success, and that information may be a matter of public record. If a person claims that profits increased by 200 percent under her watch, we should go to some lengths to find out if that's true. If he says, "During my watch we increased sales by X percent," we want to see actual numbers – reports, letters, emails, something. We need to let people know that we're going to be checking with their past employers to verify these numbers. If they don't show up for the next interview, we'll know it was all a sham. Through the years, we've seen people claim the above and more. What we've learned is that talk is cheap, and résumé talk is cheaper still.

If their claims are not matters of public record, they need to show us evidence (again, without breaking non-compete or confidentiality agreements) that explains *what they did specifically to contribute* to that success. They should be able to explain coherently whether it was due to individual effort alone or whether it was a team effort and then explain their contributions to the team effort. We've seen situations where, for example, the person was actually in the United States while the success happened in Europe. Maybe this person was just along for the ride.

If the person was the boss, we have to remember that a lot of successes happen because the boss is *not* involved, and the boss ends up taking credit for them all. Even if people provide believable evidence that the results occurred, we'll be able to see the interview come apart at the seams if they can't describe the impact of their involvement after we've asked how they contributed to it.

As we follow up on the interview, we have to distinguish between references and recommendations. *References* are provided by people the applicant chooses to give opinions of the applicant's character or passions. *Recommendations* are provided by people who are aware of what the applicant actually delivered and can give us the necessary proof.

One of the biggest obstacles to using the recommenders' knowledge fully is their concern that if they say anything, even positive, they might be sued. The solution to much of this resistance is to create a statement something like this one: "I, John Doe, release and hold harmless my prior employers _____ to share with prospective employer _____ any information regarding my past employment and performance…." As a part of the interview process, ask applicants to sign and date the statement voluntarily. When this type of release is sent to previous employers, although a few might still be too skittish to provide any information, many will respond because they'll feel that they're covered legally[2].

Most applicants will sign a statement of this sort because they want the job, and you've made this form part of your hiring process. If they won't sign it, you may be winning the battle just by asking for signatures—and being refused.[2]

---

[2] *All of this language and this process should be discussed with and approved by your professional legal counsel. This example does not constitute legal advice.*

People might want to exclude certain employers from this type of waiver. That's fine, but it has to be part of the story. "I tried to completely revolutionize this department where morale was destroyed and results had dropped 50 percent. In doing this I had to recommend a lot of changes that annoyed the powers-that-be." These stories must sound plausible and not like they're just complaining about the organization or the leadership. Remember, we're still looking for character clues, for a measure of grace.

Discovering the truth can be tricky. Some people will have had problems with every one of their past organizations because they simply are not good people. Listen for reasons. If the reasons they give reveal such things as defective character, missing passion, lack of effort, unwillingness to collaborate, or unmeetable expectations on the part of the employee, we've learned all we need to know and should run in the other direction.

On the other hand, there are good people who have worked for a number of really bad organizations (there are a lot of those out there) and just can't get a list of good recommendations from the tough people who call the shots. And there are also people who are good—but aggravating because they always tell the truth—and they might have been "blackballed" because they were fighting for a good cause in a bad place. Even aggravating people have to deliver results, however. If they're aggravating and not delivering any results, they're too focused on the negative and not on making a difference.

We don't want to become slaves to reference letters by accepting them at face value. Many of us have been asked to draft a reference letter that we really don't want to write, but we've felt some obligation. So we try to walk the tightrope: we want to sound positive for the person who asked us, and we want to sound honest for the person who will read it. We need to look for the tortured phrases and clues that this was written under some duress. Even with completely positive letters, we want to verify the facts. Every person has at least one friend, even if his dog had to write his recommendation letter. But we need evidence—whether the applicant furnishes it or somebody else furnishes it—and not just warm words.

Beyond being verifiable, the results need to be related to what people are being asked to do in our organization. There should be a *plausible stretch* from what they've done to what they say they can do, or what we need them to do, or at least to what they want to learn to do through mentoring and development in our organization. We want to offer people opportunities to grow without setting them up for likely or even certain failure. Success selling flowers doesn't mean they're going to be successful selling an intangible like intellectual property. We have to make sure their past experience is transferable into what we're asking them to do in the future.

Past performance leads to an alternative form of education, the mental intelligence and sharpness of *"street smarts,"* which people can only get in the SOHK (School of Hard Knocks). People learn the differences between what the books say and the way the world really works. They also develop the social intelligence to know when to be supportive and collaborate and when to be bold and disagree. We want to make sure they've finished this school, or at least are advancing through the grades. There are no diplomas or degrees for us to check, so we're going to have to learn about this through in-depth interviewing and checking.

It's important to have people talk for a while about *prior deficiencies* in their performance and what they learned. If they say they haven't made any big mistakes or had any failures, beware. They're either lying or they haven't done anything. Find out whether they show interest in developing skills and capacities they lack. Red flags should go up if the problems are always someone else's and the victories are always theirs.

People should also be willing and able to sift through the details to get to the core of what we're talking about. They show this through
- actively listening
- asking incisive and challenging questions
- succinctly answering questions
- asking questions of their own based on background research they've done about our organization

They should be able to provide *clear thinking* about how they might align with, and make a difference in, our organization, as well as answering questions related to our organization. For example, at Luman International, we often ask prospective employees, "What would have made your past company more effective? What potential for improvement did you see in them?" These are revealing questions for us because answering these questions is what we do for our clients. We find solutions for organizations. You can develop questions tailored to your particular market. If they can't answer these, they're probably not ready to engage passionately in the direction your organization is heading.

"NOT ONE OF THE 200 'DREAMWORKERS' WHO WORKED FOR FOUR YEARS ON THE DREAMWORKS ANIMATION FILM *THE PRINCE OF EGYPT* **HAD A 'JOB DESCRIPTION.' NOT ONE OF THEM HAD A TITLE, EITHER. WHAT THEY DID HAVE WAS AN EMPLOYMENT INTERVIEWER WHO 'HIRES THE HEART.' THE 'HEART' THAT THE SPIELBERG TEAM IS HIRING HAS THREE CHAMBERS:**

(1) PASSION AND ENTHUSIASM,

(2) CREATIVE ADVENTURING, AND

(3) RISK TAKING."

LEONARD SWEET, AUTHOR, FUTURIST, AND THEOLOGIAN [7]

At an even more basic level, we'll need to determine whether work itself is important for the people we interview. Even if what they're currently doing isn't their ultimate passion, they should be *passionate about investing themselves* into something new that might become their passion.

For example, if we're talking with a person who wants to be an architect but who is currently writing specifications, we should be able to detect a passion–and a plan–for doing architecture. Technical writing isn't his passion, but he does a good job at it because that's the type of person he is. We can sense that if he inherited $10 million tomorrow, he would begin pursuing his dream by enrolling in classes, getting experience, and advancing toward a position with an architectural firm. And the quality of work that he showed while writing specs will accompany him as he begins pursuing his true passion. On the other hand, a person without passion for a greater goal who wins $10 million will quit work the next day and start a life of leisure.

Last, what about the novices, the youngest applicants? What if a person is coming straight out of school or just hasn't lived long enough to get any serious job experience? Well, they've had other experience, places where they have performed or could have performed: academics, extracurriculars, associations, societies, part-time jobs, internships, volunteer work. There's no area of life that *doesn't* need performance and results. To find out what those were, we have to use different questions–but just as much determination.

The Warning Signs

Performance warning signs would include a lack of quality references or recommendations, an absence of verifiable results, an inability to describe how individual actions led to team or organizational results, or an inability to think clearly as evidenced by discussion or by sample letters, reports, or presentations.

If he can't think of any mistakes he's made or deficiencies he's had, that itself is a clue that either he's done nothing or he's lying. If he's done anything, he's going to have made some mistakes and uncovered some personal deficiencies.

LOOKING FOR CLUES

Make a copy of this page, and use it as a performance checklist for the next position you're trying to fill. In the meantime, go down each point related to some direct report or other current employee with whom you are struggling, and see if these critical pieces were missing.

Hard evidence of results _____

Specific contribution to past results _____

Strong references _____

Believable recommendations _____

Plausible stretch from past to future _____

"Street smarts" _____

Evaluation of prior deficiencies _____

Clear thinking _____

Passion about investing themselves _____

Clue 4: Education, Training, and Credentials

FIVE CLUES TO CONSIDER:
Character
Passions and goals
Past performance
> EDUCATION, TRAINING, AND CREDENTIALS
Assessments and diagnostic tools

The Signs of Attraction

Education and training offer another look at where people's passions are. But this means a lot more than just degrees and grade points.

What kinds of subjects have they *enjoyed studying* in the past? And *why?* Pick out the courses that look particularly interesting and unique or that tie in closely with what you might want them to do, and dig in. Why did you study this? What did you learn? How have you been able to apply it? Has it helped you in other areas of thought or action? If the answers spur an enthusiastic response, we're finding out something about what makes them tick. If we hear instead, "That was required," or "Somebody told me that class would be easy and I was carrying a heavy load," or "I needed an elective and that fit the requirements," we've perhaps learned something about absence of passion for that subject—or perhaps a lack of a coherent plan.

We want to look at their interests and what they've done in their *extracurricular activities*. Outside of schoolwork and activities, look for signs of other ambitions you can build on if they come to work with you. Can they transform what they've learned into wisdom or applicable truth about some of your current challenges or opportunities? For example, what does taking a leadership role in a volunteer position tell you about their ambition and willingness to make decisions? What does designing their landscaping tell you about their creativity?

When it comes to credentials, the "why?" questions are again the most important ones. *Why did they think this credential was valuable?* Was it worth the effort it took to get it? What have they done with it? If they could do it over, would they go after a different credential? Which one? Why?

The modern world is extremely enamored with credentials. Many of them are worthless. Others mean something, but not very much. We don't want to be afflicted with "credentialitis": we want to know if there is anything behind the parchment.

The Warning Signs

Are there any warning signs about education? Could someone have too much education? Just as 20 years of experience can actually be just one year of experience repeated 20 times, so too can education become a barrier to actual learning.

Education is a disqualifier if it has led to pride and arrogance, which always lead to ignorance, incompetence, and self-delusion. At some point, education can produce an "expert blindness" that prevents people from looking at anything in a fresh and new way.

If people are crippled by what they've learned and are prevented from thinking in innovative ways, then instead of spurring them on to further thought and development their education has become a stumbling block. If they are unable or unwilling to challenge what they've learned or to be challenged by you, they are living the fallacy that they've found the one best and true way.

For some people, education is a retreat from performance. These people hide out and continue to take courses or pursue education simply because they don't know how to perform or won't do what it takes to produce real-world results. If they don't have original research or internships or some evidence of accomplishment, they might be hiding behind education rather than using it to pursue a passion.

An overly long résumé can sound alarms. Who are they trying to impress? And why? Are they trying to convince you or themselves that they are really important? Most people with great, focused accomplishments can get their résumé on one page, and often the more the accomplishment, the shorter the résumé. U.S. President Thomas Jefferson, one of the most accomplished people of the last several centuries, did his "résumé" as an epitaph:

**HERE WAS BURIED THOMAS JEFFERSON
AUTHOR OF THE DECLARATION OF AMERICAN INDEPENDENCE
OF THE STATUTE OF VIRGINIA FOR RELIGIOUS FREEDOM
AND FATHER OF THE UNIVERSITY OF VIRGINIA**[8]

He didn't even list being U.S. President, Vice President, or Secretary of State or making the Louisiana Purchase. If he could leave these astonishing credentials out, can this applicant really need 5 pages for a non-research job?

LOOKING FOR CLUES

Make a copy of this page as well, and use it as a performance checklist while hiring. In the meantime, go down each point related to some direct report or other current employee with whom you are struggling, and see if these critical pieces were missing.

Demonstrates interests through specific training and education subject areas:
_____
_____
_____
_____

Shows interest in areas outside of education through extracurriculars:
_____
_____
_____
_____

Has important, meaningful credentials:
_____
_____
_____
_____

Has a résumé of appropriate length:
_____
_____
_____
_____

Clue 5: Assessment and Diagnostic Tools

FIVE CLUES TO CONSIDER:
Character
Passions and goals
Past performance
Education, training, and credentials
> ASSESSMENTS AND DIAGNOSTIC TOOLS

The Signs of Attraction

Something important but difficult to measure is how well someone might actually interconnect with our organization. It's a wise leader and a wise organization that uses valid, reliable assessments to get the additional insights that quantitative measures can offer, and finds other tools to get the information that can't be counted.[9]

We have to be very careful, especially with the plethora of "personality" tests floating around. If we pick a good one and use it as just *one* of *many* perspectives on a person, we may gain some value from it. But putting too much stock in these tests—thinking that we can really reduce a complex human being down to one of 4 types or "colors" or "animals" or "humors" (the original 4-part personality breakout, going back thousands of years)—is a formula for delusion and bad decision making.

Some tests are too superficial and don't tell us enough about anything to improve our evaluations even slightly. Others are based on pathologies, which may work well—if you're running a mental health clinic. Others are homespun, all-the-world-is-equally-valuable devices (like the Meyers-Briggs) that don't allow us insight into the inner challenges that can cause a new hire to fail. Almost all of them have inadequate research support behind them.[10] We'll have to work hard to find something that enlightens more than it obscures.

One revealing way to get around this problem is to use a simulation. Simulations don't have to be elaborate or expensive. For instance, at Luman International, we have potential faculty or consultants review case studies with clients' names removed and some details changed. We say, "What would you do in this situation?" While not expecting their response to be exactly what we would do, we do expect to see a similarity with the thinking processes that led us to our conclusions.

As much as possible, we want to observe people in situations similar to what they will be working in. If they're applying for a marketing position, we can give them a sample product and ask, "What would you say to sell this?" If they are applying for a clerical position and claim they can type 110 words per minute, let's have them sit in front of a computer with a timer. If they say they can do graphical presentations, we can spend 10 minutes describing a new program we want to initiate and then tell them to come back in two hours with a graphic design that makes it hard to resist hiring them.

Before making an offer, ask for a self-assessment. Ask the person to write out the "Top Ten" reasons that they want this job. You want to find out which (if any) of their passions are related to the position. We have learned incredible things from this passion self-test. If their comments are, "I like the people," "the office/plant environment seems nice," "the job is close to home," and "the benefits are outstanding," you've gotten some insight into their drivers. If the comments are more along the lines of, "I will be able to make X contribution here," "the openness is already causing me to think of fresh ways to approach several of the job responsibilities," "my experience is a unique fit with job requirements x, y, and z," and "I've never found a place more in line with my values," you've gotten a completely different insight into their drivers. You get to choose which of the passions someone expresses resonate most deeply with your organization.

> "ATTRACTING PASSIONATE PEOPLE STARTS WITH RECRUITMENT AND INTERVIEWING. WHEN RECRUITING ...LOOK AT THE WHOLE PERSON, NOT JUST THE ACADEMIC AND WORK EXPERIENCE FACETS OF THAT PERSON."
>
> DEBORAH MCINTYRE, VICE PRESIDENT-CARD SERVICES, WELLS FARGO BANK

The Warning Signs

Reluctance to take an assessment should raise flags. If they have an intelligent concern about the quality of most of the available assessments, you can tell them why yours is different. But if they leave when you assign the simulation or assessment, you know you didn't have the right person. If they do a poor job, you probably know the same thing.

Still, we need to recognize that some people might perform better under pressure and others may not. If pressure is a big factor in the position, then this is a very good differentiator and we should consider it. If not, we may want to give them a second shot at the task, perhaps with a little less scrutiny. Like people who have "white-coat syndrome," a nervousness that leads to higher blood pressure when they go to the doctor, our interviewee may need more time to relax and perhaps a second "reading" to find out what's really going on inside.

LOOKING FOR CLUES

What assessment (or assessments) are you or your organization currently using?

___

What do you like about it?

___

What do you dislike about it?

___

What do you want an assessment to determine (be as specific as you can)?

___

Who could you contact to find or construct an assessment that would help you make better hires?

_____
_____
_____
_____

Describe a position of importance to you, and jot down some thoughts about how you could do a simulation to determine potential performance.

_____
_____
_____
_____

"NOT EVERYTHING THAT CAN BE COUNTED COUNTS, AND NOT EVERYTHING THAT COUNTS CAN BE COUNTED."[11]
ALBERT EINSTEIN, PHYSICIST

FOLLOWING THE CLUES

Conduct a mock interview with one of your colleagues to practice looking for and using the 5 Clues.

Clue 1: Character

_____
_____
_____
_____

Clue 2: Passions and Goals

_____
_____
_____
_____

Clue 3: Past Performance

_____
_____
_____
_____

Clue 4: Education and Training

_____
_____
_____
_____

Clue 5: Assessment and Diagnostic Tools

_____
_____
_____
_____

> "PEOPLE ASKED TO COME AND JOIN OUR CORPORATIONS TO FIND WITH US WHAT THEY COULDN'T FIND ELSEWHERE."
> GEORGE HAINES, FINANCIAL CONSULTANT

MATCHING PEOPLE WHO SHARE OUR TEAM'S PASSION

We've come a long way together in a short time.

We've identified 5 keys to attracting passionate people and 5 major sources of clues for finding people of passion. Once we've gotten this far, we want to make sure that the passionate people we're attracting and evaluating really do share our *organization's* passion. The two most important things to determine from the beginning are:

> "OF ALL THE THINGS I'VE DONE, THE MOST VITAL IS COORDINATING THE TALENTS OF THOSE WHO WORK FOR US AND POINTING THEM TOWARD A CERTAIN GOAL."
>
> WALT DISNEY, ANIMATOR AND FILM EXECUTIVE[12]

- Do they know what our organization's passion is? Right up front, we need to ask potential hires, "What are our vision, mission, values, and stated goals?" If they can't answer that question, we know immediately that we have not identified people who understand and share our organization's passion. They are people just looking for a job. Information is too easy to access today for people to be that ignorant coming into an interview.

- Can they connect the dots between our passions and their passions? "Tell me how helping you achieve your goals will help us achieve ours?" They should know enough about our organization and enough about themselves that they can connect the dots. If they can't, the interview should be terminated, or at least postponed until they're able to come back with a legitimate narrative about the connection.

OUR VISION

In order for people to talk clearly about our organization's vision, of course, we have to have one (see ***The Passion Principle: Designing a Passionate Organization,*** the first title in the PASSIONATE LIVES & LEADERS SERIES). Does the vision reveal connection points? Does it resonate with people? Do the document and the content behind it allow people either to make a connection or not? If we've developed a vision the right way, the answers will be a resounding "Yes!" to all of these questions.

Now it's our turn. Assuming that we have a clear vision statement, we already know our vision and mission. Now we're looking at *their* vision and mission to see whether we can connect the dots. If we can't make that connection, we won't have a win-win relationship. We'll have a give-take relationship where one side is trying to help the other achieve its vision/mission/goals and the other one is not. Even if the organization is good and the person is good, that's a relationship destined to end in failure.

Consider the question we should always be asking ourselves: "How does helping this person achieve his or her individual vision and mission help us to achieve our organization's vision and mission?" We have to persist until we get a clear answer.

The Magnetism of Shared Vision

"Finding people looking for an interesting job is not too difficult," says Bill Williams, retired President and CEO of Vistage/TEC International. "Finding people who have considerable business knowledge and facilitation skills as well as a passion to help others is a bigger challenge, particularly without a large personal financial return."

Vistage, an organization dedicated to increasing the effectiveness and enhancing the lives of CEOs, has 14,000 members—all of them CEOs—in 16 countries. The company puts members together in small groups that meet for a full day each month to solve problems and share knowledge candidly—without any competitors, customers, or major suppliers in the room.

"Our key hire," Williams explains, "was what we called a 'chairperson,' someone who would run a group, manage the process, and meet with the group members one-on-one each month between group meetings. During a one-on-one meeting, the chairperson might tell a CEO, 'You need to take that issue to the group.' In group meetings, the chairperson would create a learning environment."

With nearly 600 groups meeting around the world, each group's chairperson had considerable independence and responsibility. Because membership was month-to-month, members could easily vote with their feet if the chairperson wasn't effective.

"If you can picture 14 CEOs around a table, you can see the skill level required for the job," says Williams. "The knowledge sits around that table. But the sharing and building of that knowledge, and the critique of ideas—that depends on the quality of the facilitation."

The chairperson role wasn't for everyone. The pay wasn't exceptionally high. In an organization as flat and decentralized as Vistage, there wasn't much opportunity for promotion. And even experienced executives and former consultants who took the job had to agree to keep most of their advice to themselves and focus on getting the group's members to advise each other.

"You're the king of the process, not the king of the content," Williams told the chairpersons.

"Sometimes people would sell their businesses and then want to become a chairperson for one of our groups. We'd sometimes have to say, 'No, you'd want to run these guys' businesses,'" Williams recalls with a laugh.

Getting the right people started with recruitment. *"If you want to hire a V.P. of Finance, you ask, 'Who's been doing finance?'"* says Williams. *"But for this role, we had to advertise by word-of-mouth."*

The selection process was even more important. *"We did a lot up front to get a feel for whether they could do this work,"* he says. *"We wanted them to be attracted to the opportunity for this kind of role, to get their satisfaction from helping others, to find the challenge itself exciting."*

The process included in-depth interviews, frank discussions about the mission of a chairperson, and consideration of the applicants' personal goals. *"The skills you can get from their résumés,"* Williams argues. *"What you can't get at all from a résumé is their mindset."*

Sometimes, applicants concluded, *"This isn't the right fit for me."* But those that finally came on board rarely disappointed the company or its members. This powerful approach helped to create a focused, committed organization that has made a difference for thousands of leaders.

> **"YOU HAVE TO UNDERSTAND THE MEMBERS OF THE TEAM, WHO THE EMPLOYEES ARE. YOU HAVE TO KNOW A LITTLE BIT ABOUT THEM. WHAT'S IMPORTANT TO THEM? WHAT ARE THEIR BACKGROUNDS, AND SO FORTH?"**
> FRED KOCHER, PRESIDENT & GENERAL MANAGER (RETIRED),
> AAR CORPORATION

YOUR VISION

Compare your own personal vision to the vision of your organization. Are you helping the organization achieve its purpose and reach its goals? And is the organization helping you achieve your purpose and reach your goals?

Your Vision
_____
_____
_____

Your Organization's Vision
_____
_____
_____

Similarities
_____
_____
_____

Differences
_____
_____
_____

Ways a Tighter Match Could Be Made
_____
_____
_____

Conclusion/Action
_____
_____
_____
_____

OUR VALUES

Does this person share our values?

We should have the people we interview tell us, specifically, what each of our values would lead them to do – or not do (for more on defining these values, see ***The Passion Principle: Designing a Passionate Organization,*** the first title in the Passionate Lives & Leaders series). What kinds of actions would they expect to see? Not expect to see? What would they challenge if they saw it being done in the organization? We might both have good values, but it doesn't matter if those two sets of values are not aligned. Without a match, there is no value-driven action.

For example, let's say that, as an organization, we define *fairness* as "everyone benefits in proportion to what they've contributed." But they define *fairness* as "everyone gets back the same (salary increase, benefits, etc.), regardless of what they've contributed." There's no workable way to structure a team around both of those definitions. We're expecting a team to be rewarded collectively and individually based on what each member is contributing. They're expecting all the team members to receive an equal reward, even if only one or two team members did most of the work or achieved most of the results.

Our definitions of values need to line up. Discovering these details will require us to talk with people long enough to find out whether our values align. For example, it's really easy to agree that it's good to be honest – who could be against honesty as a word or concept? But if you dig around, you can find out that some people define honesty as "it's okay to be rude as long as you're telling them the truth" or "you shouldn't take company property but it's all right to keep important points of disagreement to yourself even if the company takes a hit." Connection is in the details, not in a flowery "it's-good-to-be-good" lovefest.

If our values aren't aligned, an unraveling process will begin soon after hire. They might take our values, reshape them in their own fashion, and begin changing who we are. If they define *leadership* as "I make all the decisions"; *respect* as "you need to do what I say without a murmur"; and *trust* as "don't make any mistakes or I'll never give you anything important to do again," hiring them could turn us into a very different organization. If we let these behaviors continue, and this person seems successful, their values will be seen as the way to win.

Or we might start working on our people, subtly forcing them to give up their values or define them our way. However right we may think our values are, that's not a process likely to result in success. It's much more likely to result in people feeling like they've been twisted and contorted into something they don't like and don't want to be. That's why values alignment is vital from the start.

YOUR VALUES

Compare your own personal values to the values of your organization. Are you helping the organization live these values? And is the organization helping you to live your values?

Your Values

___

Your Organization's Values

___

Similarities

___

Differences

___

Ways a Tighter Match Could Be Made

___

Conclusion/Action

_____
_____
_____
_____
_____

Semper Fi: The Enduring Bond of Powerful Values

"It was a country in anarchy," says Colonel Mike Chené, recalling his tour of duty as a company commander in Somalia. "We were in eastern Africa, in a place we'd never seen before. Rival gangs had tried to take ownership of the country. There were crops rotting on the vines outside the city. People were afraid to gather their crops or replant because gangs would shoot at them or execute them."

The Marines, says Chené, were in Mogadishu with one simple message for the terrorized civilian victims of this chaos: "The U.S. is here."

Carrying that message meant that the 200 Marines under Chené's command had to uphold American values in a dangerous, challenging place. Many of them were as young as 18.

To ensure that Marines would act on the Corps's values—including the value memorialized in the famous motto semper fidelis*—officers started by setting an example. "You never put a Marine into a situation or position you'd never been in yourself," says Chené, a veteran of several combat missions. "We didn't just tell people to do things. We were out there in front of them doing the same thing. It separates our military from every other military in the world."*

Next, Marines had opportunities to act on the values they'd observed. "The strong learning experiences that we give our Marines put their wise decision-making skills into very realistic situations," Chené observes. "We have a non-commissioned officer corps with command and leadership capabilities. I told them, 'I'm not always going to be there watching you. You have to make the right decision based on your training.'"

Chené remembers one day when his young Marines went above and beyond that expectation. They were patrolling the streets in Mogadishu, and periodically, someone would shoot at them. Most of the time, Marines with professional training faced a minimal threat from armed amateurs. "It wasn't constant combat for us," says Chené. "The gang members weren't very disciplined or very good soldiers. They would shoot wildly over our heads."

But that day, one of the patrols had a chance to embody the virtues of honor and discipline that had been ingrained in them. They were riding through tight streets with close-quartered alleys and cinderblock buildings no more than 2 or 3 stories high.

"It's hard to comprehend," Chené explains, "but there was a woman holding a child, a young child—a year or so old—and a guy grabbed her to protect himself. At first, he was on his knees behind her, and then he sprawled out on the ground underneath her, sniping at the patrol."

It was a tense moment, one in which twenty young men could easily have put themselves out of danger by engaging with the gunman. It took extraordinary discipline for them not to shoot back.

"I was talking to a corporal on the radio, and he said, very calmly, 'These guys are terrible shots. We want to leave it alone so we won't endanger a civilian. We'll go back and get him later, sir.' With all the guys under his command, this 19-year-old thought through it—and on their own, they realized that ending the situation would put a woman and child in unacceptable danger," Chené remembers.

The patrol was authorized to protect itself, but as they had assessed their position, the young Marines had seen that they had a decision to make. "Instead of engaging, they decided to take cover and call me up so we could figure out what to do," says Chené.

"That's when I realized that these men were capable of far more than I had even thought," he remembers. Seeing their values in action—their discipline, their honor, and their sense of duty in protecting themselves yet understanding their mission to protect civilians—gave Chené pride in being a Marine that has never been surpassed—not in the 27 years he spent in the Corps.

"How can you not be proud to be in an organization such as this?" he says. "All they want is to do their job right. They are patriots. They are proud young men. And it's just an unbelievable privilege and honor to serve with them."

THE MATCH

THE BIG QUESTION IS WHETHER OR NOT WE HAVE "THE MATCH."

Would this person *really* fit in our organization? Is this the right kind of person with the right kind of vision, mission, values, behaviors, and goals to align with ours? People may be very good on their own, but do they align with the kind of slot, team position, and people that we already have on our team?

It's important to evaluate not just skill sets but also the structure of the position.

We don't want to lock a "people person" in an office. We don't want to give a team player a solo flight. We need to be candid in our assessment of how this person will fit this situation. People are adaptable and can often accommodate even excruciatingly painful jobs, but that's a lot different from loving the work and doing it with fire. Passion seldom grows out of accommodation–out of trying to make something fit that won't fit.

Beyond that, we need to recognize that there are distinctly different kinds of teams. At Luman, we don't talk about "team building." We talk about *TeamsBuilding*™—building multiple kinds of teams to fit the work being done. When someone talks about being a "team player," they usually mean that the person tries to cooperate (and often mean he or she won't rock the boat), but the real question is "On what kind of team are we asking this person to play?" We could have a person who is aligned with our vision and values and equipped with the right skills, and we could *still* blow it by putting them on the wrong *kind* of team. We always need to match people's work styles to the purpose and work environment of the team.

Another factor is the style of the leader to whom a person will be reporting. A very high percentage of people leave jobs even when they like the organization and what they're doing because they can't work with the person directly above them. It *might* be because the leader is a jerk or the employee is an idiot, but it might just be a personality mismatch: a very detail-oriented boss over a creative personality who can't stand somebody breathing down his neck all the time, or a very laidback kind of boss with somebody who says she prefers a lot of structure and direction.

If you've found someone who aligns with your organization in every other way but doesn't fit this position, leave that person's file out on your desk until the right position opens up.

> "WHEN YOU TAKE ON A PARTNER, AND WHEN YOU SELECT EMPLOYEES, BE SURE TO CHOOSE PEOPLE WHO SHARE YOUR PASSION AND COMMITMENT AND GOALS. IF YOU SHARE YOUR MISSION WITH LIKE-MINDED SOULS, IT WILL HAVE A FAR GREATER IMPACT."
>
> HOWARD SCHULTZ, STARBUCKS FOUNDER AND CEO[13]

KEEPING AND DEVELOPING PASSIONATE PEOPLE

So where are we? We've found passionate people, made sure they matched up well with who we are as an organization, and ensured that we're moving in the same direction. We've got the people equivalent of gold, if not platinum.
So how do we *keep* these people? And how do we, and they, get the most out of their work?

Even great organizations are facing more and more turnover as the "Baby Boomers" retire or move toward retirement, leaving fewer people to replace them. And the generations coming behind them are even pickier about where they'll work and why. But this isn't a bad thing if we've got a good thing going.

We're going to do a better job of finding passionate, performing people, and we're going to do a better job of keeping and developing them, and that is going to give us a *huge* competitive advantage. And the big, stupid organizations that offer lots of money, but little or nothing else of the Attraction Principle, are going to find themselves much less able to buy and drain souls.

So when we find really great people, what are we going to do to hang on to them? We don't just want to retain them with good pay and benefits and a good title, or through inertia. We want to retain them, and more: we want to retain *who* they are – their passion, their commitment, their investment in our organization.

We want to keep their fire blazing. We want them constantly thinking and working to change and develop our organization. That means, first of all, that we're going to have to consider developing people as a full-time process and not as a 2-day or 2-week-a-year event that they get out of the way so they can "do their job."

Learning by Passion

At Luman International, one of the deficiencies we have found in many organizations is that they only allow people to learn new things that are "job-related."

But what is job-related? The Chief Technology Officer of Microsoft once was asked what he studied to stay on top of his game. You'd expect him to say, "I read *Bits & Bytes Quarterly* and *Computer Molecules Today*." But no. He said that he studied *history* and *biography* to develop his skills, to learn how a great organization like his could continue to succeed or slide toward failure. He explained, "As the Internet begins to hook us all together, you look for precedents to help figure out what will happen next."[14] He had learned that a great organization can profit from knowing what other great organizations have done in the past either to maintain their success or to fail.

So were history and biography "job-related" for him? Absolutely. Job-related learning is anything our employees are passionate about that develops their ability to think, to bring new ideas or new tools to their current or future positions. We suggest that you let learning follow people's passions.

We want to help people develop skills to act on their passions, rather than trying to create passion where none exists for current skills and duties. Both are important – we surely want them to be excited about what they're already doing – but we want to find out what else they're passionate about that they're not currently doing. That's where the learning should take them.

Development is part of the job. Developing the people who work for and around her should be a primary expectation of a leader. Leaders should constantly be looking for new ways to develop people – through formal training, informal learning opportunities, coaching and mentoring possibilities, and "stretch" assignments.

It's one of the best ways to ensure that we keep passionate people – people who are also continually growing in their ability to add and create value. Someone has said, "Worse than training people and losing them is *not* training them and *keeping* them." We'll get a lot back for our investment in people, even if at times the length of the return period is short.

10 KEYS TO KEEPING AND DEVELOPING PASSIONATE PEOPLE™

Passion, like anything high-energy, can dissipate over time. Over several decades of research, Luman has found that there are 10 Keys to maintaining high levels of passion in people.

Leaders can design and build passionate organizations. And they should. The organization's overall environment is the first and most important factor in keeping passionate people. It has to be conducive to nurturing passion, and just won't get the job done if it is missing one or more of the *10 Key Elements of a Passionate Organization*™. People simply won't stay if the organization is lacking *Passion DNA*™. (To learn about this, see **The Passion Principle: Designing a Passionate Organization,** the first title in the Passionate Lives & Leaders series).

But the environment is only part of the equation for success. Another critical part is having leaders who can deliver on the *10 Keys to Keeping and Developing Passionate People*™. Leaders of even one or two people can implement these 10 Keys. If we want to win hearts and minds—and keep winning them—we need to make sure that we consistently offfer these 10 Keys.

Not everyone will weight or value each of these 10 at the same level as someone else. For example, I might think the third one is the most important, and you might think the eighth one is most important. But all 10 of these are vital to maintaining passion in every human being.

HERE ARE THE 10 KEYS:

Key 1: Sense of Freedom

Let freedom ring. People have to really believe and understand that they are *free* – free to make suggestions, make decisions, change processes, make mistakes without getting hurt, challenge the status quo, or come up with new and better ways of doing things. And they need to do it in an atmosphere where these actions are not only permitted but welcomed and rewarded.

Key 2: Sense of Ownership

People need to be able to say, "What I'm doing here belongs to me; I own it. I'm pretty good at it and want to keep doing it." If they feel like cogs in a gigantic machine–and perhaps faulty cogs at that–most people will be unable to engage passionately in their work.

> ### *The Miracle of Involving Everyone*
>
> *Starting with a hotel housekeeping team that was "doing bathrooms on the graveyard shift," Jorge Norena has invited people with whom he works to take ownership. Time and time again, this revolutionary approach has expanded both the bottom line of the organizations for which Norena has worked and the passion of his teams.*
>
> *Working for the housekeeping department of a 5-star hotel in Dallas early in his career, he created his own programs for cleaning. His investment in the hotel's success captured the owner's attention, and she told him, "You know, George, I would like to equip you and put you through school." Norena enrolled in night school and graduated as a Certified Hospitality Housekeeping Executive.*
>
> *"Housekeeping is the biggest budget and staff of a hotel," he explains. After taking over the housekeeping department of a large hotel, he needed to find ways to trim costs. "I came up with an idea: instead of complaining, why don't I empower the housekeepers to do the savings for me, to have ideas to reduce the cost for me. I gave them the ownership and the incentive. It worked miracles."*

The first week Norena was at the hotel, the staff was able to reduce towel usage by one towel per room by telling guests, "If you don't want your room cleaned every day, let us know." They saved hundreds of thousands of dollars while being environmentally friendly.

The quality of service also needed an overhaul. When Norena first took over the department, he faced grim numbers: nearly half of the comments the hotel had been receiving were negative. "People weren't happy, mainly with the service and with their interaction with employees." Clearly, he needed a way to give the housekeeping staff a stake in the hotel's reputation going forward.

The solution came to him from an unexpected source.

"I was watching TV one day, and I saw the show The Price Is Right," he remembers. "I started a program called 'The Fine is Right.' I gave people $5 each week, and I took out money for each thing done incorrectly: 'If you forget to put in toilet paper, that's 25 cents; if you didn't change the linen, that's 50 cents.' The program ended up only costing us about 75 cents a day per person."

At the end of the year, 92 percent of the comments were positive, return guests had increased, and the hotel was only spending an extra $1000 a month on the program—which was more than offset by the savings and the increased business.

"That program made it all the way into the hotel 'bible' used to teach hospitality students," Norena reports.

That success allowed Norena to carry his ownership approach to new places. Walt Disney World recruited him to take on the role of Director of Housekeeping for the Contemporary Resort, and after dozens of interviews, he was hired—a rare outside hire in a company known for promoting from within. In his first year, the hotel saved $3 million. Norena's innovative programs were written up and published in about 120 countries, and universities and hospitals around the world wanted to borrow his approach.

"Most of us want to find money first, and then we try to find passion for the activities that give us that money," says Norena, who has since started several successful companies and served as a lay pastor to a Hispanic congregation in California. "I learned a long time ago that if you get passionate about what you want to do first, the money will come along. It will be the by-product of commitment."

For the people who work for Norena, getting a genuine stake in the organization means that money really does come along when they invest their passionate commitment.

Key 3: Boss Devoted to Your Future

When most people talk about their bosses they discuss issues like these: "Do you get along with your boss? Does your boss give you fair evaluations?" Not bad, but we want to suggest some other very important questions: "Is your boss passionate about your success? Is she passionate about your future? Is he thinking about how to develop the people who work for and around him?" To paraphrase Mike Murdock, people will go where they're celebrated, not where they're tolerated. People want bosses who celebrate them.

If one of your direct reports can't be passionate about the success of one of her people, it's time to reassign that person to a leader who will actually be devoted to his success. Not, "I'm willing to develop the person," but, "I'm passionately devoted to this person's future and will do what it takes to develop it." This means ensuring that people get into positions that have upward mobility, even if it takes them away from that current boss. Great leaders don't hoard their people. They try to find places where people can be even more passionate, deliver higher levels of value and results, and feel better about their lives—even if it means the leader takes a short-term hit and has to train somebody new to do the job.

> "INDIVIDUALS KNOW WHETHER THEY ARE CONTRIBUTING OR NOT. THEY ARE NOT FULFILLED IF THEY ARE NOT REALLY CONTRIBUTING, AND PEOPLE KNOW THAT BEST WHEN THEY ARE WHERE THEY ARE SUPPOSED TO BE. IT IS OUR JOB AS LEADERS TO HELP THOSE INDIVIDUALS AND STUDY WHAT MAKES THEM TICK."
>
> DAVID GREEN, CEO, HOBBY LOBBY STORES

Key 4: Opportunity to Take Risks

Passionate people need opportunities to try new and difficult things. Different people have different risk levels, but everybody needs to know, "I can branch out and invest myself in an innovation that might end up changing the future for my organization (or team or unit)." This is more than freedom – this is having the clear authority, resources, and organizational support to take a big, new step.

Key 5: Mutually Set Goals

Everyone understands that the organization has goals that will be communicated and then translated into expectations. But if people are really going to invest their passion, they need to feel that they participated in setting those goals. They have to know and believe that they had a voice, that the goals really belong to them and were not simply dictated from above.

Key 6: Clear Expectations & Feedback

"I don't know what I'm supposed to do, and I don't know if I did it or not." Too often people leave organizations because of confusion over expectations and feedback. Some people might be able to guess expectations intelligently. Others might be self-analytical, and as long as they feel they're doing a good job, that's enough. But you don't want to bet on people being able or even willing to be detectives. For many people, clear expectations and feedback are critical components of a fulfilling work environment, and deal breakers if they're absent.

Key 7: Access to Resources (Including Upward Access)

For people in engineering, science, manufacturing, or IT, resources are an obvious and basic need. But all of us need to have access to the resources required to do our jobs. Those resources include upward access—the ability to get decisions and information in a timely way. Access to resources sends people the message that the organization and its formal leaders are supporting them in doing what they've been asked to do—and, they hope, what they *want* to do.

Key 8: R&R&R (Respect & Recognition & Reward)

The 3 "Rs." To have high levels of passion, people have to be given more than the typical recognition and rewards. They need an important element that is so often missing: respect. If people have respect from their bosses, a very small recognition or reward means a lot. If someone *doesn't* have that respect, a lot of applause or money still won't make that person feel appreciated.

Key 9: Challenges That Stretch Without Stressing

In his book *Good to Great*, Jim Collins talked about "BHAGs" – big, hairy, audacious goals. Giving people BHAGs will challenge them to avoid two of the great drains on organizational life—boredom and fatigue. People have to be stretched, not only to perform but to feel like they're growing and succeeding. We don't need to apologize for stretching people, even though we have to be on guard that we don't stretch people so far that we stress them out. Great leaders always monitor the stress levels of their people. But for their good, we should stretch people constantly with bigger challenges – challenges that grow the organization while pushing people's skills to the next level.

Key 10: Shared Vision & Values & Trust

There has to be an ongoing sense of shared vision and values and the trust that results from living them together. People can't just agree one time with a plaque on the wall and then let the effect on interactions and decisions evaporate. Our vision and values and the trust that they create must be reflected in the organization and its people on a daily basis. (To learn about this, see ***The Passion Principle: Designing a Passionate Organization,*** the first title in the PASSIONATE LIVES & LEADERS SERIES).

APPLYING THE 10 KEYS

Because we're talking about keeping and developing passionate people, we encourage you to give this list of 10 Keys to each of your employees and ask them to rank them (not rate them): Which one is most important? Which one is next most important, which one is third most important? And so on. All 10 are important, but you now have a golden tool: an individual "passion retention plan" for each of your people.

For example, if Olivia has "Sense of Freedom" as her top key, you want to put her in situations that are not restrictive, where she's not boxed in, where all the rules are not set out in advance. You should give her lots of latitude on methods and processes. You might, at the same time, be overseeing Stan, who has Sense of Freedom as his last-ranked Key. With him, you can leave a few more restrictions in place without producing the same response you would have received from Olivia.

If someone has "Sense of Ownership" as their least critical Key, you can probably let them finish up 90 percent of a project and then put somebody else on to finish up the last details. But if that's somebody's most critical Key, you'd better let that person stay on the project until it's fully done.

If somebody has "Clear Expectations & Feedback" as the highest-ranked Key, set up a project plan and do a review every other day. Let them know what's expected at the next phase and tell them how you think they're doing on the current one. If they rank it last, you can safely go longer–perhaps much longer–between updates.

Using these 10 Keys means we're constantly putting our people in a position to accomplish their work passionately.

How important is this? In one study, 77 percent of customers surveyed said they stopped doing business with an organization because of employee attitude.[15] If our people aren't passionate–if we can't attract, hire, keep, and inspire passionate people–how can our *customers* be passionate about us? And how will we stop our customers or clients from leaving us?

COMPARING THE 10 KEYS

Go back to Attraction 4 (on page 13), where you noted your first ideas about what these Keys might be.

Where were points of similarity? What does this tell you about the criticality of these Keys?

_____
_____
_____
_____

Where were points of difference? Would you change your opinion now that you've actually seen the 10 Keys? If not, what would you add to the 10 Keys from your list–and which of the 10 Keys would you delete to make room for your addition?

_____
_____
_____
_____

RATE YOUR ORGANIZATION

On a scale of 1 to 10, rate your organization on each of the keys, considering the organization's ability and willingness to offer new hires or team members each of these 10 Keys. A rating of 1 means there is no evidence of this key in your organization, and 10 means your organization exemplifies the key trait.

Sense of Freedom	1	2	3	4	5	6	7	8	9	10
Sense of Ownership	1	2	3	4	5	6	7	8	9	10
Boss Devoted to Your Future	1	2	3	4	5	6	7	8	9	10
Opportunity to Take Risks	1	2	3	4	5	6	7	8	9	10
Mutually Set Goals	1	2	3	4	5	6	7	8	9	10
Clear Expectations and Feedback	1	2	3	4	5	6	7	8	9	10
Access to Resources	1	2	3	4	5	6	7	8	9	10
R&R&R	1	2	3	4	5	6	7	8	9	10
Challenges that Stretch without Stressing	1	2	3	4	5	6	7	8	9	10
Shared Vision, Values, and Trust	1	2	3	4	5	6	7	8	9	10

Now, jot down why you assigned each score and what could be done to improve it.

Sense of Freedom _____

Sense of Ownership _____

Boss Devoted to Your Future _____

Opportunity to Take Risks _____

Mutually Set Goals _____

Clear Expectations and Feedback _____

Access to Resources _____

R&R&R _____

Challenges that Stretch without Stressing _____

Shared Vision, Values, and Trust _____

> "A SOUND SYSTEM OF MEASUREMENT, RECOGNITION, AND REMUNERATION DOES NOT REWARD COUNTER-CULTURAL BEHAVIORS - HOWEVER SUCCESSFUL PEOPLE MAY SEEM IN THE SHORT TERM."
>
> PETER LAVERS, MANAGING DIRECTOR, CUSTOMER FUTURES

"GIVING PEOPLE THE OPPORTUNITY TO GO BUILD SOMETHING, GO CREATE SOMETHING, GO WORK - IF YOU LOOK AT GROWTH AND QUALITY OF OUR SERVICE, OUR GROWTH HAS BEEN ENORMOUS IN THE LAST 12 TO 15 YEARS. AND THAT IS THE RESULT OF A BUNCH OF PASSIONATE PEOPLE IN KEY POSITIONS LOVING WHAT THEY REALLY DO."

JAMES B. DESTEFANO, PRESIDENT & CEO, OCCUPATIONS, INC.

TEAMING PEOPLE OF PASSION

It's amazing to see how different teams perform against expectations.

4

Some teams have very talented team members and produce nothing. There is either no passion–"Oh, no, another team meeting"–or the passion comes out in negative ways like criticizing or silencing teammates, fighting for credit and turf, and complaining about goals and nitpicking processes.

Other teams have people with average skills and abilities and deliver outstanding results. You can feel the passion when you walk into the room. People are interested, involved, focused, and committed.

What's the difference? Well, anyone who has lived in organizational life for very long knows that there are probably 50 ways for teams to be dysfunctional, dead, and done. But both positive and negative outcomes start with having the right (or wrong) people on the team. Great team goals and processes can't overcome poor matching and bad chemistry.[16]

First, we'll talk about how to go about teaming people of passion to deliver passionate performance. Then we'll give you a quick overview of the *7 Keys to Effective Teams*™ so you can consider ways to build all of your teams effectively from the inside out.

THINGS TO REMEMBER WHEN TEAMING PEOPLE OF PASSION

Whether we're adding someone new to our organization–a team in the largest sense–or to a team within our organization, we have some things to do to help us ensure a successful teaming. Here's your teaming checklist:

- **Diversity Review** – We're talking here about diversity of *thought*. It's hard to be effectively passionate when everyone thinks the same way (although it's easy for them to get on a wrong track and believe in it zealously). You want each team member to feel that they are bringing a unique perspective to the team, so that they can commit the best of who they are to the team's success.

- **Charter Commitment** – Have the person review the Team Charter (You have to have one! For more information on how to draft a Team Charter, see ***The Passion Principle: Designing a Passionate Organization,*** the first title in the PASSIONATE LIVES & LEADERS SERIES). Dig into the details and see how well the team's primary passions and values resonate with the potential team member's passions and values.

- **Role Commitment** – Are they ready to take on the strong roles we've outlined for them? Contribute in discussions and meetings? Make decisions? Show initiative? Take ownership and accountability? Take responsibility both for their own individual contributions and for the whole team's success?

- **Team Type Analysis** – Given who this person is and what her passions are, does she really fit the type of team you're building? Is this an individualistic team, in which all members are expected to do their jobs with great freedom and initiative, or a coordinated team, in which all members are restricted in their decisions and actions by some or all of the other team members? A maverick personality could be a great fit for the former and a disaster for the latter.

- **Team Interviews** – No one is smart enough to analyze all aspects of a current team to determine whether a potential new member will fit. Have everyone on the team talk with this person, ask questions that get down to character and passions, and then have a heated conversation about "the fit." If it's a team being formed from scratch, develop an interviewing team to perform this task.

TEAMING REVIEW

Take a look at your team through the above lenses. What adjustments would be helpful for your current team or for the time when you add a new member?

Diversity Review:

Adjustments to current team: _____
_____
_____

Specific actions to take with new team members: _____
_____
_____

Charter Commitment:

Adjustments to current team: _____
_____
_____

Specific actions to take with new team members: _____
_____
_____

Role Commitment:

Adjustments to current team: _____
_____
_____

Specific actions to take with new team members: _____
_____
_____

Team Type Analysis:

Adjustments to current team: _____
_____
_____

Specific actions to take with new team members: _____
_____
_____

Team Interviews:

Adjustments to current team: _____
_____
_____

Specific actions to take with new team members: _____
_____
_____

7 KEYS TO EFFECTIVE TEAMS™

Now let's take steps to ensure that any teams we form (or are part of) will "deliver the goods."

Since we want our teams to win, and for all team members to be victors, here are the 7 Keys in an easy-to-remember acronym:

VMVB™
Intelligence
Cohesion
Tools
Openness
Results
Sustainability

Let's look briefly at each these:

1. ***VMVB*™** – This stands for Vision, Mission, Values, & Behaviors. We have to develop a team charter that answers questions about team purpose, direction, critical success factors, and acceptable actions and interactions. The charter should stir passion and bring full alignment. It's at its best when it's developed by the whole team and represents its diversity. (To learn about this, see ***The Passion Principle: Designing a Passionate Organization,*** the first title in the Passionate Lives & Leaders series).

2. ***Intelligence*** – Does the team have a *Strategic Planning Guide*™? Do we have the necessary time, space, and forums for thinking, reflecting, and focusing? Do we take *PitStops*™ to see if we're spending our time on the right things and avoiding distractions? Without design, most teams are dumber than their least-intelligent member. With design for thinking, teams can operate with a higher-order intelligence. (To learn about this, see ***The Thinking Principle: Using Passion to Innovate and Create Value,*** the third title in the Passionate Lives & Leaders series).

3. ***Cohesion*** – Effective teams have to be formed organically, not mechanically. To have cohesion, teams need to have a boundary between them and everything that is not part of the team. But the boundary needs to be permeable, so that necessary communication and support can go both ways. Systematically eliminate "turf," silos, and other artificial mechanical barriers to collaboration. And keep the team challenged: nothing works better to bring a team together than a goal that can't be achieved without the whole team's best effort.

4. ***Tools*** – Effective teams have specific tactics that they can use to assure the full presence throughout the team of *powersharing*™, commitment, initiative, responsibility, ownership, *unavoidable accountability*™, and ways to stir *constructive dissent*™ and deploy *consensus management*™.

5. ***Openness*** – Teams die when communication dies. This death can be due to poor leadership (leadership that doesn't both set the tone and insist that everyone be transparent), lack of trust, lack of courage, lack of passion (important to get that one right with all team members), or just plain smarts (people are too smart to speak up if they take a beating for it the first time).

6. ***Results*** – It seems obvious to say that teams need to have a focus on results, but it's amazing how often they don't. It is very easy for teams to be sidetracked by peripheral goals, politics, "lowest-common-denominator" thinking, and operating in a reactive mode to changes imposed by the hierarchy or market. To assure success, teams need to have a symbiotic relationship with change, innovation, risk, and mistakes.

7. ***Sustainability*** – Nothing is more ordinary than for teams to start off great and then deteriorate over time. Teams need to have a systematic approach to evaluating themselves, refining their actions and interactions, and continuously improving their performance. And the team will have to force itself to face, define, align with, and (where possible) change current reality. (For more on this, see ***The Reality Principle: Exploiting Change and Crisis with Courage and Passion,*** the seventh title in the PASSIONATE LIVES & LEADERS SERIES).

There you have them. If you build these 7 Keys into your team design, you'll have a terrific start on addressing the 50 dysfunctions of a team.

A Straight Shooter

When Colonel Cagley was 10 years old, at the height of the Korean War, he decided he was going to become an army officer, and he set his sights on West Point. Although he didn't ultimately go to West Point (he was appointed but couldn't pass the physical), he achieved his childhood goal of becoming an officer. Cagley attributes this success to a high tolerance for the risk of telling the truth and to an appetite for responsibility.

As a major in Heidelberg, Seventh Army Headquarters, Cagley worked for Major General William Dykes, a man who knew how to get the people he commanded to take the risk of speaking up. Cagley recalls the day that Dykes called him in to tell him, "Major Cagley, your job is to be the psychological operations officer for this, the Seventh Army. You are to make your best judgment. Present me with the facts. Do not try to guess what I want you to tell me. I want you to tell me the truth and your best judgment of the needed course of action. Then, if I don't agree with you, you support me, unless I'm doing something illegal and you know it's illegal—and then you'd better correct me."

It was a lesson that stuck with Cagley throughout his 37-year career in the U.S. Army. In fact, truth-telling was a piece of a larger leadership imperative: the duty to take responsibility for the unit's success.

"If you want to be in charge, you want the responsibility," he says. "There's a big difference between being in charge and simply being in command."

Cagley put his passion for unvarnished truth and leadership responsibility to work in military intelligence, in assignments "behind the scenes and in dark basements," as he describes it. Within that field, he gained expertise in developing units and planning the creation of new reserve organizations.

"A unit is like a baseball team," he says. "You can have 9 outstanding baseball players, but if they don't work together, you're never going to win anything. Eisenhower wasn't a great military genius, but he was very good at knowing what generals to put in what position to do what job."

Cagley developed the people who served under his command and put them in positions where they could succeed.

"I had 6 majors who worked for me on my staff, and 3 of them went on to retire as general officers," he says. "I'm so very proud of that because I was able to mentor them. I gave them a section to direct or a study to do, like a military intelligence research study." Cagley remembers one major who became especially adept at developing battle plans and operations and then predicting how the Soviet Union would react.

"I wouldn't nitpick," he says. "I'd give direction, and if I thought they were going in the wrong direction, I'd bring them back onto the course. Mostly, I gave them the power to make their own decisions, to give their own input, and to be original in what they did."

Cagley also kept a list ready of people in his unit who should receive various advanced trainings so his officers and non-commissioned officers could take advantage of other units' unused training funds at the end of each year. As a result, his people were the most highly trained of any of the reserve units stationed in Heidelberg.

For Cagley, developing a high-performance unit was a chance to pass on what he'd been given. "It's like what Gen. Dykes did for me," he says. "I told my people, 'Don't try to guess what I want you to do. Just do your best job and give me the results.'"

> "PASSIONATE PEOPLE SEEK OUT AND FIND OTHER PASSIONATE PEOPLE....ONE OF THE BEST DECISIONS I MADE WAS TO HIRE ONE EXTREMELY PASSIONATE MANAGER. WE HAD TWO CANDIDATES FOR THE POSITION, ONE WITH MUCH BETTER EXPERIENCE, BUT HE PRIMARILY WANTED THE JOB AS A METHOD TO MAKE MORE MONEY. THE SECOND WAS SO EXCITED ABOUT THE OPPORTUNITY THAT HE WAS WILLING TO TAKE A CUT IN PAY JUST TO GET THE JOB. WE ENDED UP HIRING THE SECOND CANDIDATE (AND OF COURSE GAVE HIM A BIG PAY RAISE, TOO). IN THE FOLLOWING MONTHS THIS PERSON WAS THE BEST RECRUITER WE HAD IN THE COMPANY... HE HELPED US HIRE DOZENS OF PASSIONATE NEW MEMBERS TO OUR TEAM."
>
> KURT MCCASLIN, PRESIDENT & GENERAL MANAGER, ANADARKO (BRAZIL)

EVALUATE YOUR TEAM

Evaluate your team on the 7 Keys. On each of these, give yourself a grade (A, B, C, D, or F (for "Finding our way out of the team wilderness"), give yourself a time frame for improvement to the next-higher grade (or to an A+ if you gave yourself an "A"), and then make a note on things you can do immediately–whether you're the team leader or not–to improve.

KEY FACTORS	GRADE	TIME FRAME FOR SOME IMPROVEMENT	NOTE
VMVB™			
Intelligence			
Cohesion			
Tools			
Openness			
Results			
Sustainability			

TIME FOR ACTION

Finding passionate people is hard; keeping them may be even harder. But with what we've discussed in this book, you can find and keep passionate people and create an organization in which people fully invest.

Better to attract and keep one passionate person than 10 smart duds. For the organization and for you as a leader, the passionate person is a gift to the future.

For more on developing the passionate people you have brought into your organization, see ***The Influence Principle: Communicating and Coaching to Ignite Passion,*** the eighth title in the Passionate Lives & Leaders Series.

FAQ

Isn't it okay to have some people who aren't passionate, who just plod along and do their jobs?

Yes, if you want to have a mediocre organization. How many duds does it take to drain the life out of an organization or team? Not many. Every job, no matter how mundane it might seem to others, can be done with passion by someone who really cares about it.

What should we do if we have someone on the team who isn't passionate about our organization and what we do?

You can't put in what's missing with other human beings. Encourage them to find a place of passion for them and wish them a passionate farewell.

What if we have someone who has a lot of passion, but it always comes out negative?

This might be a good person who has been burned by the organization or people and has had her idealism turn to cynicism. Or he might be a nasty person. Give these people a chance, in a limited time frame, to trade their negative passion in for the good stuff. If they just don't want to be good people, assist them with remote career planning.

We don't look at passion at all when we're hiring, other than to notice whether people seem outwardly enthusiastic (which most interviewees do). What do we need to do?

First, you need to make it a high priority. Then you need to ask very specific questions about passion and rate them on their answers. Luman can provide help if you need it, with questions and ratings that can be folded into any hiring system.

How do we get HR on board with this?

Most of the people I've met in HR departments are good people who are trying to do right by their organizations. But the profession hasn't focused (up to now) on finding passionate people, and our friends in HR have a ton of responsibilities in addition to recruitment and hiring. Share this book and your take on it with them. And by all means, start doing this in your own area right away.

How do we get around the problem of people faking enthusiasm in the interview?

The problem with many interview processes is that they're processes: we go through the steps and make decisions, even if we don't really know enough to make them. We need to interview long and deep enough to see what these people really care about, how they really think, and how all of that matches up with who we are and what we need.

What do we do with an interviewee who doesn't seem to know a lot about us?

If there is a legitimate reason, which in the day of easy research is hard to imagine, send the person away until he can come back with a narrative about why he's going to be good for you and you're going to be good for him. If there isn't a legitimate reason, you just got some time back for other things, since this interview should end very quickly.

Could it be good to use the 10 Keys to Keeping & Developing Passionate People™ during the interview process?

Absolutely. It was originally designed for use with existing team members, but this is another fine way of determining who people are, what's important to them, and whether that's a match (for example, you expect people to be very independent and they rank "Sense of Freedom" tenth). It also is a great statement about your focus on passion and on providing the framework for that passion to flourish.

I really like the 7 Keys to Effective Teams™. Is there a way to learn more on this?

Luman has an in-depth, 1-day (and of course, passionate) course called "Leading Passionate Teams."

My team is ineffective and struggling. Should I start making modest changes or should I do major surgery?

There are two issues here: potential and expectations. On potential, if most of the basic elements are there but we're missing some important ingredients (for instance, a few key people, a team charter), there's no reason to disband the team and start over. But if the potential is limited, you can spend a lot of your life and energy trying to tweak wires on a car that needs to go to the junkyard. Expectations can change the equation. If they are modest, modest changes might get you there (as long as the potential is good). But if the challenge is great, you need a great team to meet it and you probably won't get there with minor modifications. If the great challenge has a restricted time frame (often the case), the temptation is to stick with a passionless, underperforming team because "we don't want to change horses in the middle of the stream." The problem is that some horses may never make it to the other shore.

Can't you coach for passion?

No. You can change the design of an organization or team to make it more passion-friendly, and you should. You can work hard to put people in a place where their passions and the organization's needs and passions line up. But if you've done these things and there's still no fire, you can coach until doomsday without success. As my friend Pete Luongo says, "I can help make you better than you are, but I can't help make you different than you are."

How critical is this "Attraction Principle" to long-term success?

It's critical for a number of reasons. Two big ones are: First, passion is the switch that turns on our ability to optimize financial, technical, and other capital; and second, the world has changed and organizations that focus on this are going to be able to draw the "believers and winners" in a world where they're much in demand and short in supply.

For more on this powerful subject of passion, please see James Lucas's full-length book **The Passionate Organization:** *Igniting the Fire of Employee Commitment.*

Luman International also has an in-depth assessment, the Passion Quotient™, which will provide you tremendous insight into your organization's Passion DNA, Infrastructure, Leadership, People, and Transformation/Adaptive Capacity.

We offer a full-day course, "Leading Passionate Teams," and a number of keynotes or short presentations on the topic, including "Igniting Your Team's Firepower™."

We can assist you on several aspects of designing and building a passionate organization, with our Signature Processes, including "TeamsBuilding™" and "Developing Consensus Management™ and Constructive Dissent™."

"JIM LUCAS'S BOOK IS A BRILLIANT COMPENDIUM OF TRENCHANT OBSERVATIONS ABOUT THE RELEASE OF THE HUMAN SPIRIT. THE ULTIMATE WEAPON FOR THE 21ST CENTURY."
ARTHUR D. WAINWRIGHT, CHAIRMAN & CEO, WAINWRIGHT INDUSTRIES, INC. (WINNER OF THE MALCOLM BALDRIGE QUALITY AWARD)

For more information, please visit lumaninternational.com.

Endnotes

1. *Drucker, Peter.* The Effective Executive. *New York: HarperCollins, 2006.*
2. *Hoover, John and Angelo Valenit.* Unleashing Leadership. *Franklin Lakes, NJ: Career, 2005.*
3. *Emerson, Ralph Waldo.* The Works of Ralph Waldo Emerson. *"Character." Roslyn, NY: Black's Readers Service.*
4. *Quoted in Noah benShea.* What Every Principal Would Like to Say. *Thousand Oaks: Corwin Press, 2000. Grenville Kleiser (1868-1953) was the author of 5 books, including* Make Your Life Worth Living.
5. *At Luman International, we have developed the Power and Performance Scale™, a rating system with out-of-the-ordinary questions and categories to evaluate performance. The scale allows an analysis of whether the person has demonstrated results, or only listed "roles and responsibilities." This and other assessments are available for licensing. Please email Maryl D. Janson at mjanson@lumaninternational.com for more information.*
6. *Sweet, Leonard.* Soul Tsunami. *Grand Rapids: Zondervan, 1999.*
7. *"Brief Biography of Thomas Jefferson (1743-1826)."* Monticello, Home of Thomas Jefferson. *February 2003. Thomas Jefferson, Foundation, Inc. Accessed 7 July 2008. Available: http://www.monticello.org/jefferson/biography.html.*
8. *Clifford, Stephanie. "The Science of Hiring." Inc. August 2006: 90-98.*
9. *For a devastating inside look at personality tests, see* The Cult of Personality Testing *by Annie Murphy Paul.*
10. *From a sign Einstein had hanging on his wall at Princeton University.*
11. *Collins, James Charles and Jerry I. Porras.* Built to Last. *New York: HarperCollins, 1994.*
12. *Schultz, Howard, and Dori Jones Yang.* Pour Your Heart Into It. *New York: Hyperion, 1999.*
13. *Stipp, David. "The Idol of the Geeks: What They're Reading in the Computer Biz," Fortune 3 March 1997.*
14. *"Why Customers Defect."* Delight or Defection. *Fenton, MO: Maritz, 2006.*
15. *In the book* The 5 Dysfunctions of a Team, *the author mentions absence of trust, fear of conflict, lack of commitment, avoidance of accountability, and inattention to results, but doesn't address the other drivers of team failure, including this most-important question, "Who are we teaming and will it work?" Other deal breakers that we address at Luman include mission clarity, diversity of thought, prioritizing, selection of the right type of team for the mission, Powersharing™, quality of leaders/leadership, proactivity, and ability to face and align with reality.*

JAMES R. LUCAS

James R. Lucas is a recognized authority on leadership and cultural design. He is a groundbreaking author and thought leader, provocative speaker, and experienced consultant on these crucial topics.

Jim is President and CEO of Luman International, an organization which he founded in 1983. This firm is dedicated to Developing Passionate, Thinking, Pure-Performance Organizations™ and their leaders, people, and teams.

Clients are from sectors as diverse as health care, pharmaceuticals, medical devices, financial services, accounting, energy, chemicals, forest and paper products, transportation, computer hardware, diversified manufacturing, consumer products, diversified business services, construction, state government, and federal government. They range from Fortune 1000 public companies and private for-profit organizations to not-for-profits and government agencies.

Jim has written numerous curricula for business and leadership seminars, as well as many essays and articles. In addition to the PASSIONATE LIVES AND LEADERS series, he is the author of five other landmark books on leadership and organizational development:

- High-Performance Ethics: *10 Timeless Principles for Next Generation Leadership*
- Broaden the Vision and Narrow the Focus: *Managing in a World of Paradox*
- The Passionate Organization: *Igniting the Fire of Employee Commitment*
- Balance of Power: *Fueling Employee Power without Relinquishing Your Own*
- Fatal Illusions: *Shredding a Dozen Unrealities That Can Keep Your Organization from Success*

Prior to founding Luman International, Jim was President of EMCI, a high-tech design and manufacturer of aerospace systems and medical devices. Before that, he held managerial and executive positions at Hallmark Cards, VF Corporation, and Black & Veatch Consulting Engineers.

Jim is an award-winning senior faculty member of the American Management Association, where he served for several years as a charter member of the Faculty Advisory Council. He taught its premier course, The Course for Presidents (in which he was and is the highest-rated faculty member), and is the overall highest-rated faculty member in the history of the AMA. He is also a frequent presenter at the Center for Leadership & Executive Development. Jim has an extensive speaking schedule, in which he addresses topics from his books and research, and has been interviewed frequently on radio and television.

Jim received his education in leadership, business, economics, and engineering at the University of Missouri (Columbia and Rolla), where he received his Ph.D. (h.c.). He has also taught at Rockhurst University. Jim is past president of the Academy of Engineering Management, a member of the American Society for Training and Development, a member of the American Society of Engineering Management, a senior member of the Society of Manufacturing Engineers, and a registered professional engineer in Missouri and Kansas.

Jim has been honored with continuous listings in *Who's Who in America* (1999-2009), *Who's Who in the World* (1989-2008), and *Who's Who in Finance & Industry* (1989-2009).

PHIL HOTSENPILLER

Phil Hotsenpiller is an executive coach who brings his wealth of professional experience, creativity, and spiritual insight to passionate leaders around the world.

Phil is the founder and President of New York Executive Coaching Group, a firm that has assisted Presidents, CEOs, and other professionals to achieve breakthrough results in their professional and personal lives. His clients are a diverse and accomplished array of leaders in many sectors: arts and entertainment, finance and industry, and religious and not-for-profit.

Phil is also the Executive Director of the not-for-profit International Freedom (IF). IF is working with its partners to build 200 education centers for Dalit children and 200 vocational training centers for Dalit women throughout India. Using the power of documentary film, International Freedom also seeks to raise awareness among Hollywood "influencers" of the plight of the Dalit people in order to bring about lasting change. IF's acclaimed documentary, DELETES, was selected to compete in the Artivist Film Festival and the HollyShorts Film Festival, where it earned the Audience Choice Award. In addition, IF has recruited more than 1000 volunteers to serve urban Los Angeles, feeding the homeless and creating after-school programs and health clinics.

Throughout his career, Phil has worked extensively on issues at the nexus of leadership, artistry, and spirituality. Previously, he served as adjunct professor in a division of Southern Theological Seminary and Union Theological Seminary. He has spoken on leadership and theology throughout Mexico, Brazil, Paraguay, El Salvador, Honduras, Guatemala, Romania, Yugoslavia, and France, working with the European Team of Christian Associates International in the area of leadership development. He was one of 25 selected to serve on the Pastors Task Force for the War on Drugs organized by former U.S. "drug czar" William Bennett. Phil also founded *One Purpose*, a weekly television show on WSFJ-TV and a daily radio broadcast on WRFD radio.

Phil continues to address these issues, facilitating a weekly group of 100 prominent actors and young leaders in the Hollywood entertainment industry. With bestselling graphic novel artist/illustrator Rob Liefield, Phil is a founding partner of 12 Gates Productions, an entertainment company producing a full line of graphic novels, lithographs, DVDs, feature-length films, and video games. He currently serves as Teaching Pastor at Yorba Linda Friends Church in Southern California; YLFC was recently honored as one of the 100-fastest growing churches in the United States. As a leader of discovery trips to Europe, Phil teaches European history, art, philosophy, religion, and culture in Geneva, Amsterdam, and Aix-en-Provence. These trips provide participants with an understanding of different cultures and build bridges between passionate people around the world.

Phil received his education in history, religion, political science, and English literature at Southwest Baptist University. He earned his Master of Divinity from New Orleans Baptist Theological Seminary and completed postgraduate studies at Christ Church College, Oxford University.

Phil is married to Tammy Hotsenpiller, author of *A Taste of Humanity* (2009) and co-founder and designer of Humanity™ for All, LLC, a cutting-edge clothing line noted for its original art with an urban flair and its strong links with dozens of social justice organizations. Songwriter Tye-V (Nycolia Turman) is writing lyrics for an upcoming Humanity™ album.

THE PASSIONATE LIVES & LEADERS SERIES

Book 1 - The Passion Principle: *Designing a Passionate Organization*
Book 2 - The Attraction Principle: *Finding, Keeping and Teaming Passionate People*
Book 3 - The Thinking Principle: *Using Passion to Innovate and Create Value*
Book 4 - The Paradox Principle: *How Passionate Leaders Merge Competing Ideas*
Book 5 - The Performance Principle: *Delivering Results through the Power of Passion*
Book 6 - The Confidence Principle: *Discovering Your Life's Passion and a Place to Live It*
Book 7 - The Reality Principle: *Exploiting Change and Crisis with Courage and Passion*
Book 8 - The Influence Principle: *Communicating and Coaching to Ignite Passion*

You and every member of your organization will be inspired by this 8-book series, in which real-world leaders share their experiences in building passionate teams and organizations. Read how the ultimate competitive advantage is harnessing the passion that leads to outstanding performance!

For more about **THE PASSIONATE LIVES AND LEADERS SERIES,** *visit www.livesandleaders.com.*

To order, or to learn more about volume discounts for individual books and sets, visit Quintessential Books at www.quintessentialbooks.com.

To learn more about implementing these principles, visit Luman International at www.lumaninternational.com

READ BOLDLY. THINK DEEPLY. LIVE PASSIONATELY.
www.quintessentialbooks.com

Patsy Campbell

Baptist Publishing House

Pray, Work, Win!
Baptist Publishing House
ISBN 0-89114-360-2

All Scripture quotations, unless otherwise noted, are from the *Holy Bible, King James Version.*

Copyright © 2004 by Baptist Publishing House. All rights reserved. No part of this publication my be reproduced or transmitted in any form or by any means, electronic or mechanical, including photocopy, recording, or any information storage and retrieval system, without permission in writing from the publisher. Requests for permission to make copies of any part of the work should be mailed to: Permissions, Baptist Publishing House, Post Office Box 7270, Texarkana, Texas 75505-7270.

Printed in the United States of America.

Dedication

This book is dedicated to *each* one of you who has faithfully prayed for me on this maiden voyage into writing. I never thought I would have this experience, and I feel sure this is my alpha and omega.

This book is dedicated to *each* one of you who asked me, "How's it going?" "How far along are you?" "Is it getting any easier?" or just said, "I'm praying for you." I needed each word of encouragement and the nudge it gave me to press on.

This book is dedicated to the Women's Missionary Auxiliary at every level. Thank you for the many opportunities you have given me to do work for the Lord and receive the victory.

Pray
When God said pray, I said, "Oh, Lord, not today." But then I learned when God says pray, I say, "Dear Lord, I will obey."

Work
When God said work, I said, "Oh Lord, I can't, I'll shirk." But then I learned when God says work, I say, "Doing God's labor, in obedience, is true joy, and not *just* work."

Win
When God said win, I said, "Lord, I've just never been in a *lucky* place." But then I learned when God says win, it's not by luck, but by His *amazing grace*.

Contents

Dedication 3
Epigraph 4
Preface 7
Acknowledgments 9
Section One — Pray 11
Persist 13
Get Real 31
Affirm God 45
Yield 53
Section Two — Work 55
Willing 57
Organized 65
Risk 69
Kinds 75
Section Three — Win 85
Wise 89
It's All About You, Lord 93
Never Give Up 101
Epilogue 107

Preface

This book was written as a study guide for Women's Missionary Auxiliary groups and any other groups in the church, or as a personal study you can use alone and at your own speed. It is all about *praying, working,* and *winning.*

Salvation by God's marvelous grace must come first. Prior to salvation or being born again, we are not in the family of God. God is not our Father, nor Christ our Savior. In this condition we cannot have prayer fellowship with God.

No lady will be the prayer warrior she needs to be without grace. No lady will put her shoulder to the wheel and get involved in her God-given ministries without the new birth. And surely no lady will be one of God's race-running winners without God's free gift of salvation. So be, as the old hymn title says, "New Born Again."

John's gospel is about believing and receiving. *"For God so loved the world, that he gave his only begotten Son, that whosoever believeth in him should not perish, but have everlasting life"* (John 3:16). *"These are written, that ye might believe that Jesus is the Christ, the Son of God; and that believing ye might have* [receive] *life through his name"* (John 20:31).

Right now, stop, and make sure of your salvation. Are you sure of your salvation? Do you know you have truly been born again? If you can answer yes, you are ready to proceed with this study. If you must answer no, my prayer is that you will seek help to know Jesus personally through the salvation experience.

Here is the plan of salvation.

- Know that God loves you and wants to give you a new life. *"For God so loved the world, that he gave his only begotten Son, that whosoever believeth in him should not perish, but have everlasting life"* (John 3:16).
- See that your sin has separated you from God and the life that He desires to give you.
 "As it is written, There is none righteous, no, not one.... For all have sinned and come short of the glory of God" (Romans 3:10, 23).
- Realize that Jesus Christ died for you, was buried, and rose again so that you might have eternal life.
 "God commendeth his love toward us, in that, while we were yet sinners, Christ died for us" (Romans 5:8).
- Confess your sins to God and turn away from them to serve God faithfully.
 "Repent ye therefore, and be converted, that your sins may be blotted out" (Acts 3:19).
- Receive Jesus Christ by faith, accepting Him alone as your Lord and Savior.

"If thou shalt confess with thy mouth the Lord Jesus, and shalt believe in thine heart that God hath raised him from the dead, thou shalt be saved" (Romans 10:9).

Now let's proceed. You may be wondering how long this study will go on in your life. It will continue until the rapture or until God takes you home through death. What you study and discover in this book must be put to practice *every* day in your life. There will never be a day when you do not need to talk to your heavenly Father. I love the saying, "A day hemmed in prayer is a lot less likely to unravel." You will never live a day when you do not need to be at work in the Lord's vineyard. You should want to be like Jesus, and one of His traits was that He did the work God had called Him to do.

In Luke 2:49 we read: *"And he* [Jesus] *said unto them, How is it that ye sought me? wist ye not that I must be about my Father's business?"* So must we be! There will never be a day when we do not need to feel the blessings of accomplishment.

Read and savor Matthew 25:21, *"His lord said unto him, Well done, thou good and faithful servant: thou hast been faithful over a few things, I will make thee ruler over many things: enter thou into the joy of thy lord."*

Come on. Dig in. Let's grow!

Acknowledgments

Eureka! God has helped me finish the manuscript. It is January 18, 2003. That's cutting it pretty close. This has been a hard journey for me, but God has let me grow so much. My fellowship with my heavenly Father has truly deepened from this experience.

The WMA committee considered me! Truly amazing! I was just floored, speechless in fact, the day Lucille Hutto told me, "We want you to write our study book for 2004." I sat there, mouth open, unsure. Thank you for asking. Today, I am so glad I said yes.

I belong to the digital divide. I just thought I would write this in longhand and send it along to the publishing house. Jerome Cooper, however, gently made it plain that this was not the case. What to do? What to do? Then God provided the answer. Her name is Glenda Tipton. She came to my rescue, even volunteered to do so. I could not have done this without you. Thank you *so* much!

Jerome Cooper has been very helpful the times I have talked with him. Now that the book is finished, I'm sure we'll have more conversations getting it printed. Thank you for help in the past and the future as we get this project completed.

Thank you in advance to each one who reads *Pray, Work, Win*. My prayer is that you will truly receive a blessing from the study and will experience great growth in your Christian life.

Love and prayers,
Patsy Campbell

Section One — Pray
Persist
Get **R**eal
Affirm God
Yield

The most important decision you will make in all of your life is to accept Jesus as your personal Savior. Your second most important decision will be to have a *strong,* daily commitment to prayer.

Write your salvation experience in the following space. Be very specific. Be ready to share it with a partner at your next meeting.

_____
_____
_____
_____
_____
_____
_____
_____
_____
_____

Write out your thoughts about the opening statements concerning the importance of salvation and prayer. Have a short discussion in your WMA or women's ministry meeting to allow the ladies to share their thoughts.

_____
_____
_____
_____

Chapter 1

Persist

Becoming the prayer warrior that both God and you desire to be requires persistence. The dictionary defines *persistence* as: "to keep on doing; to last on and on; to continue obstinately." Let's look at the meaning of *obstinate*: "clinging to one opinion or purpose; not easily subdued or removed; stubborn."

Comment on what *to persist* has to do with prayer.

_____

_____

_____

❑ Yes ❑ No Is persistence biblical? Find at least three Bible verses as references. Write them here.

_____

_____

_____

_____

_____

_____

_____

_____

_____

_____

Read 2 Thessalonians 3:13. *"But ye, brethren, be not weary in well doing."* Comment on this verse.

_____

_____

_____

_____

Pray, Work, Win!

Are you engaged in well-doing when you pray? Record your answer here.

_____

_____

_____

At your next group meeting, share and comment on the scriptures each of you have discovered concerning persistence. In order for you to accomplish this desired goal of a close relationship and fellowship with God, you will need:

- A daily time
- A daily place
- Your prayer tools: Bible, hymnal, journal, study books, devotional books, *Gleaner*, state paper (for me *The Baptist Trumpet*), your church bulletin, pen, pencil, highlighters, eraser, other items you discover you need.

Now let's consider these requirements one at a time.

The daily time

"Every day, Lord? You know me well, Lord, I might commit three days a week, but seven? Lord you know how busy I am. My mornings are hectic; I'm at work at noon; my evenings are for family, going to church, and other activities. I don't waste my time. Lord I'm retired. You know I love you and want to be a prayer warrior, but, Lord, when I get everything else done and start to pray, I fall asleep."

OOPS! What does this sound like? It reminds me of the song "Excuses" that our children sing. We are so prone to rationalize about why we can't pray instead of asking God to give us commitment to pray daily.

❑ Yes ❑ No Does God ever make excuses with you?
❑ Yes ❑ No Does He ever put you on hold?
❑ Yes ❑ No Does He ever take a call waiting and stop listening to you?

Write your thoughts here on the comfort you receive knowing that twenty-four hours a day God is always available to you.

_____

_____

_____

_____

Patsy Campbell

List two or three of your main excuses that block your *daily* prayer life.

_____

_____

If you cannot make and consistently keep your daily time with God, the place and tools will not be needed. You must really desire this daily fellowship. You must believe in its importance to your life as a child of God. You must come to embrace the fact that a strong, daily prayer time will produce great growth in you. What are some things that you are willing to do to make sure you meet God every day at the appointed time?

_____

_____

When you fail to keep the appointment, and you will from time to time, what measures will you take to get *immediately* back on track?

_____

_____

Deciding on your daily time is very personal. What works for one won't work for another person. John Maxwell has a great study entitled *One Hour With God*. As I did this study for myself, the one hour worked for me. You might do this study to help you get disciplined to praying daily.

Why is self-discipline so hard?

_____

_____

_____

Why is self-discipline so necessary?

_____

_____

_____

How much time do you want to commit? The time must be of such duration that you can really talk to your heavenly Father. Your time must be more than

Pray, Work, Win!

just a moment to pray "save the lost and heal the sick." Work out the length of time you need to be specific. At this time (and it will change as you commit), how much time would you like to set aside each day for your prayer time?

_____

Why did you choose this particular amount of time?

_____

_____

Again let me emphasize that this amount of time is what is just right for you and your heavenly Father. No one system works for all and you will find your time by trying several approaches. Perhaps you want to try two or three short times each day, such as fifteen minutes each time. A thirty-minute session in the morning and another thirty-minute session later in the day or at night could work for you. One hour may be just right for you. Will you be one of those who rises an hour before the rest of the family and prays? Trial and error will help you work out the time that is just right for you. Try one time for awhile and then another; it's okay to take a while to get your time just right. This will turn out to be your most important time of the day, so work on it until you get it just right for you.

What are some things in your life that will hinder your daily prayer time?

_____

_____

How will you commit to fight these things?

_____

_____

_____

_____

The daily place

"Same time, same place, *every* day, Lord?" That's right. The daily place is very important also. You do not want to be interrupted. If you are home alone at your prayer time, consider not answering the phone (just a thought). When others answer the phone, have them take a message for you. Remember, God stays in His place and does not interrupt your prayer for *anything*. This commitment is a must if you are going to develop an intimate, deep bonding with your heavenly Father.

You may want to pray at a desk or in a chair near a table so you have a ready place for all your tools, which I will talk about later. You may want to choose a special prayer nook, and when you go to that place, it is *only* to pray. You may want to hang appropriate pictures and quotations, and these could change from time to time as God leads you to new thoughts and ideas.

You may try out several places, then pray in earnest and let God lead you to the *best* place. I have two places, one is in a park where I can look out at the Arkansas River, and the other is in my den at home in my recliner. Both of these places have become so important to me because these are my places to commune with my heavenly Father. Certainly I talk with God in other places as well, but I am more intimate with Him in these two places. I'm more real; I am more honest; I get more personal; I pour out my heart to Him holding nothing back. I do go to these two places for other reasons than praying, but I always feel differently about them when I am there for prayer. So ask God, seek the place, and find the one(s) just right to meet your prayer needs.

When you find that place, go there every day. Hold nothing back, and say, "It's just you and me Father. I've come to fellowship with You, I've come to just abide in You. I've learned that I always grow and come away just a little different." This time with God is really about fellowship and abiding. Please spend just a little time here to do the following exercise and think about your answers.

What is a relationship with Jesus?

_____

_____

_____

_____

When does the relationship begin?

_____

_____

_____

Will you ever lose the relationship? Give scripture to support your answer.

_____

_____

_____

What is fellowship with Jesus?

_____

_____

Pray, Work, Win!

Will you ever lose/break this fellowship?

_____

_____

What are some things that can break fellowship?

_____

_____

How do you restore broken fellowship?

_____

_____

What does it mean to abide in the Lord?

_____

_____

Right here, I want to strongly recommend the book *Secrets of the Vine* by Bruce Wilkinson. I used this book in my daily prayer time and have read it more than once. I underlined in it, made notes in the margin, wrote about it in my journals, and have used it several times in talks I've been privileged to give. I really learned so much about abiding from this book.

One verse of scripture has truly become my desire. *"As the hart panteth after the water brooks, so panteth my soul after thee, O God"* (Psalm 42:1).

Why is it important to abide in the Lord?

_____

_____

_____

Your prayer tools

The time is set; the place is set! Begin your daily prayer time as you go about the task of choosing *your* tools. The tools I listed earlier are the ones I use. You will choose your own tools over a period of time, and they will work for you. (I promise they will.) As you look at my list you may think "Good grief, if she uses all that stuff, how does she get any praying done?" That's just it! This is *my* list of tools; it works for me. I do not use all my tools every day, but I want them all with me so that if I do want one, I'm not interrupted by getting up and going after something. Remember, the devil does not like this daily prayer time. He is not standing on the sidelines cheering you on. Rather, he is thinking of every way possible to hinder you, yes, interrupt you. He knows if you get interrupted, you may not get back to praying. Remember what we said about *persist*.

The tools change from time to time. I can't tell you how many different tools I have used, finished with, or returned to use again. I find the Lord does lead me back to certain tools and I find in them dear old friends. The lessons I have forgotten flood quickly back. I see clearly that what I forgot is the very thing God wants me to remember. So enjoy the tools and change them as often as God leads you.

This can become a tedious session and the devil can really get the victory right here. Don't let that happen! Stop right now and use the power of prayer to ask God to help you be receptive. I cannot emphasize enough upon you how important the tools are. They have just blessed me beyond what I could ever imagine. Years ago when I set aside my time and place, I began to experiment with the tools. At first I was clumsy. It took me a good while to get comfortable with this process. Now I know what I am doing and I know the next study book I will use. Right now my devotional book is *Grace for the Moment* by Max Lucado. It was a gift and has turned out to be a gold mine. I can't tell you how many precious nuggets I have dug out in four months. I have eight months to go before I will have to choose a new devotional book, and God may lead me to just do this same one again to dig deeper. So have fun, experiment, and get comfortable with your tools.

Will you use all your tools every day? Some days you will, most days you won't. Do you need more than one journal? I don't know. That depends upon what works for you. I use three different journals. Can you add to or delete from these tools? Every day, if you want. Over time, you will find this becomes very easy. You will know just what you need at the time. This is *your* prayer time, *your* talking time with God. If you are using all these tools all the time, how will you ever have time to pray? Just keep experimenting and it will all work out.

Some days most of your time will be spent praying. Some days you may not have an entry for your journal, and some days you will spend more time on your devotional. Some days you will spend more time just listening to the heavenly Father, just abiding and letting His love envelop you. Trust me on this. Your own routine will develop; it will all just begin to work out right and what a blessing this time will be in your life.

Frustrating, huh? Mind boggling to say the least! No. Just keep experimenting, simplifying, and, most of all, keep trusting God to work this out.

Pray, Work, Win!

I keep my tools in a large basket by my recliner, very handy. When I go to the river, I choose the ones I will use and take them with me. My prayer tools have truly become my friends. I am comfortable and unencumbered by them. Oh, how many blessings have come through this system, and how much God has taught me through this method of organization and efficiency. It keeps me from wasting this precious, precious time I have with my Lord. *"Let all things be done decently and in order"* (1 Corinthians 14:40). I believe this verse applies to your daily time alone with God, as well as other areas of your life.

Once more, don't let this step become a burden. These are your tools. Choose what you want and reject what you don't want. You can start by getting a large empty basket and let it hold *nothing* but your quiet time tools. If you choose to sit behind a desk, empty a desk drawer, or choose some other receptacle that works for you.

Let's discuss one tool at a time. You may choose and reject or keep changing over the years as your quiet time deepens, gets richer, fuller, sweeter — and it will, I promise!

Bible

This is your most important tool so choose it wisely. There are many, many excellent Bibles you will want to check out. Really examine several Bibles and chart your finding. After careful consideration, make your choice(s). Remember, make it work for you. The only caution I would offer is that too many translations can be too tedious. For my personal quiet time, I use only two. I use many translations at various times, but only two for the daily quiet time.

At this point, you will need to stop and go to a good Christian bookstore. This will take time and may take several trips. You may want to talk with a salesperson for advice. Fill out the following chart.

My Bible research chart. Include as many Bibles as you want. Ask to see a list of the ten current best-selling Bibles, perhaps you will just do those ten. I would like you to start with the *Scofield King James*, then do the ranking after completing the entire chart.

The scripture I choose to research in each Bible is: (write out passage here.)

As I wrote this section, I spent some time remembering just how much I enjoyed doing this exercise and there are many new editions out now. I think I'll find some time to go update my list.

After completing this chart, go back and rank your entries from your favorite to your least favorite — 1, 2, 3, etc. I think that one Bible to choose for sure in your personal quiet time should be the King James Version to check for accuracy.

Title	Likes	Dislikes	Cost	Rank
1. Scofield Ref. Authorized KJV				

Pray, Work, Win!

Why is the Bible your most important quiet time tool?

_____

Bible(s) chosen! Praise the Lord! Another victory. My tool basket now has something in it, so let's move on.

Hymnal

A hymnal may not be a tool you want in your basket and that is fine. I love music and find that it really helps in my personal quiet time and worship. I have quite a few different hymnals, so I change from time to time. I really get so much from the words of the praise choruses that I bought a book of those and use it at times for my hymnal. You can sing or *joyfully noise* the words; God hears it as a sweet, sweet sound in His ear because it comes from one of His children. You could pray the words as well. Try this activity. You might find it a real blessing. If not, discontinue it. Remember, nothing cumbersome.

What is your favorite hymn and why do you like it?

_____

_____

_____

What phrase in the entire hymn do you identify with the most and why?

_____

_____

What praise chorus is your favorite and why do you think it speaks to you?

_____

_____

Yea! Add the hymnal to your basket! (Progress!)

Journal

A journal is one of my favorite things! Journals come in all shapes and sizes. You can use one at a time or several. You can write in the journal daily or as the Lord leads.

My *prayer journal* is an eight and one half by eleven inch loose-leaf binder which lets me add and delete pages as necessary. Oh yes, I throw pages away when I am through with them. I have been doing this for years so imagine how bulky this journal would be if I didn't throw away pages. My prayer journal is the same thickness it has been from the beginning. I do use this journal every day in my quiet time. If you decide to use a prayer journal, and I sincerely hope you will, set it up the way you want it. It is your journal. Experiment. Try out different methods until you find one that works for you. This method works for me. I have my journal in nine sections with a title page for each section and a tab on each title page for easy access. I do not want to waste time hunting through the journal each day. My sections are: (1) Everyday, (2) Sunday, (3) Monday, (4) Tuesday, (5) Wednesday, (6) Thursday, (7) Friday, (8) Saturday, (9) Praise & Thanksgiving for answered prayer.

Why these sections? Well, I have several things I pray for every day. I go to the *everyday* page first, then move to the page for that day of the week. I find there are so many prayer needs I can't pray for each one every day, so I have daily pages and try to have about the same number of requests on each page. Some everyday requests will be moved to a weekday page when it is no longer urgent. When you no longer need to pray for an item, delete it. You constantly keep adding and deleting to keep your journal up-to-date. This system helps you to pray more effectively and not to overlook things you need to be praying about. Then you surely will want to give praise and thanksgiving when a request has been granted. How thrilling to look over these blessings and see God's grace and graciousness at work. How awesome it is that God loves me so much that He hears and answers me. How this affirms to me just how much power there is in prayer! I love the praise section.

I was once in a workshop on journals, and the leader shared one journal in which the Wednesday page was devoted entirely to her grandchildren; she had several. There was a picture of each one with very specific requests under each picture. These requests changed often as the children were growing and their needs kept changing.

Set your prayer journal up to suit you. It is very personal and needs to be shared only with God. You may show your journal to others if this is comfortable for you, but you certainly have the right to keep it private.

My *quotation journal* is a beautiful journal, given to me by a friend, that I set aside for quotations; people who know me well know I am a quotation nut. This is in my tool basket, but I do not use it every day. As I am writing this section, I'm reminded that it has been a while since I used this journal, but it is very helpful when preparing a talk. How is this journal set up? Remember our old pals *decently* and *in order*? I love this journal and want it to work for me. I don't want to flip through every page to find what I need. In the margin of the title page I have a list of contents for the whole book. I left ten pages for each topic and tabbed the pages. The first section is titled *Proactive*; the second is *Prayer*. So far I have nine sections. There is still room for additional sections as the Lord leads. I have so enjoyed this journal, and there might not be a single other person who would ever want one on quotations, but it works for me.

I use my *personal jottings journal* often, but not every day. Sometimes I only write a sentence or two, and some days the jottings are lengthy. The notes might be on a scripture I have been studying, or my thoughts on current personal study or devotional materials. On many Mondays I feel led to do

Pray, Work, Win!

jottings on Sunday's sermons. Make notes about anything on your heart.
Journaling has just become a way of life for me. It has taught me so much about me, and it has really helped me to abide in the Lord. I sincerely believe you will find journaling to be life-changing. Make it work for you so it truly is a blessing, not a burden.
Design your journals by what the Lord lays on your heart based on your personal needs at the time. One lady journals about life lessons God has taught her; she has grown so much from it.
Have you ever kept any kind of spiritual journal(s)?

If yes, what were the subjects?

_____

_____

What has been the greatest reward/blessing you have received from keeping a journal?

_____

If no, why have you never considered being involved in journaling?

_____

Do you think keeping a daily prayer journal would improve and deepen your prayer life? How?

_____

_____

_____

_____

Study books

You will find hundreds of choices for study books, so don't be overwhelmed. Ask God, "What subject do you want to teach me next, Lord?" Be sensitive to your personal needs at the time. Someone may suggest a great book to you, but its subject is not your current struggle or the timing is just not right. Months or even several years later God may lay that same study book on your heart because the timing is right. You may not use your current study book every day. This method is a great way to discipline yourself to study. From study God sends growth.

Let me suggest some study books that have blessed my heart and enriched my life. This is certainly not a complete list. I'm sure you will think of many others. You may have read a book that blessed your heart and now you want to use it as your study book for your quiet time.

- *Experiencing God*, Henry Blackaby
- *One Hour With God*, John Maxwell
- *The 7 Habits of Highly Successful People*, Stephen R. Covey
- *Boundaries*, Dr. Henry Cloud and Dr. John Townsend
- *Don't Just Stand There, Pray Something*, Ronald Dunn
- *Prayer*, E. M. Bounds
- *The Prayer of Jabez*, Bruce Wilkinson
- *Secrets of the Vine*, Bruce Wilkinson
- *Praying God's Word*, Beth Moore

I would suggest, since this study is an effort to get you to begin and remain faithful to a daily personal prayer time, that your first study book be on the subject of prayer.

I want to share one of my study experiences which really convicted me to pray God's Word back to Him, and for years now I have been praying the scriptures more and more back to God. It has been such a deep blessing in my life. Now this is not just simply praying the verses back as written, but making them personal to fit your situation that day. Praying the scriptures is not for God's benefit, but yours as you discover things you did not know about yourself and gain understanding of how to apply the scripture to your life.

My life verses are Philippians 4:6-7, *"Be careful for nothing; but in every thing by prayer and supplication with thanksgiving let your requests be made known unto God. And the peace of God, which passeth all understanding, shall keep your hearts and minds through Christ Jesus."*

The last few years of my working life with the school district were pretty hectic. Student problems had become more serious and occurred with much greater frequency. I began to pray these verses to God every morning as I was driving to work. I prayed them word for word just as they appear above. It was a great help and comfort to me.

I attended one of John Maxwell's seminars, and while there bought his book *One Hour With God*. I was almost finished with my current study book and felt led to study on prayer again. This study changed the way I prayed these verses to my heavenly Father. He had given me these verses a long time ago for a reason; praying them to Him became very personal. The words were true intercession for myself. "I have needs. Lord help me."

Pray, Work, Win!

Below is the journal entry I wrote. I give you this to help you to see what I mean, not to brag or boast. Many could write a better example, but I hope this helps you to begin to pray the scriptures.

My life verses — my way

"Dear Father,

I want to talk to You again today about my life verses. I just can't seem to be anxious about *no thing*. I am anxious about many things. Lord, I don't want to be anxious, worried, frustrated, or fearful because this shows a great lack in me; it says I don't trust You enough. Forgive me, Father, I do so love and trust You and would never have You think otherwise. Help me to come to You and talk over everything. Everything! Help me to be persistent and deeply earnest until I get Your answer. Lord, how I thank You for what You have taught me in this scripture about thanksgiving. I have learned to thank You for the answer before I ever stop praying, because I know it will be forthcoming. I can't begin to tell You, Father, just how life changing that has been for me and how much it has increased my faith in You. Thank You for sending me Your peace to my heart and mind every day. This peace of Yours, Father, really passes my understanding. I truly don't see how things can be so stormy with such warring factions, yet in my heart You have sent such sweet peace. I just know You have, and I thank You and praise You for it.

In Jesus name and for His sake. Amen"

I don't know exactly why God led me to share this with you, but I know it was for me because I have had some anxious moments about writing this book. As I was sharing with you, God was sharing with me. We had a wonderful worship experience, and His peace has once again overcome my anxiety. "Thank You, Lord."

Please ask God to give you your life verses. This may take a while, so be patient and wait on the Lord. When he does give them to you, write them here.

My life verses

_____

_____

_____

_____

_____

Pray them for several days just word for word from the Bible. When you feel led to do so, record your prayer from these verses and from your heart in your own words. It will be *very personal*.

Patsy Campbell

My life verses — my way

_____
_____
_____
_____
_____
_____
_____

From time to time, you may feel led to change verses. I have asked the Lord over the years about this and will continue to do so. God, so far, has confirmed the Philippians passage as my life verses and they serve me well. I pray many other scriptures to the Lord, but my life verses I pray almost every day.

Thump! What is that sound? Why, bless your heart, you are putting your journals and study book in your tool basket. Looking good!

Devotional books

Devotional books are optional items and you may want to omit them if it becomes too much to add to your quiet time. I do this when I find something outstanding. Remember, I mentioned *Grace for the Moment* by Max Lucado. I was working on a two-hour teaching session on grace for the state WMA seminar and began reading an entry each day but *not* during my quiet time. After about two weeks of those entries every day, I transferred this book to my tool basket and have been using it *in* my quiet time ever since. I have made several journal entries about these devotionals. The thoughts are very short and can be read in only a minute or two. Once, when reading the subject "God Is Crazy About You," I tucked that thought away for a talk I was preparing for a later date. What you use in your quiet time can have far-reaching applications. Another thing to consider is letting the devotional and the study book be one and the same.

Why are these called devotional books? *D-E-V-O-T-I-O-N.* Do some jottings right here on your devotion to God. This exercise may be somewhat painful, but it will also be very rewarding.

_____
_____
_____
_____

Pray, Work, Win!

Read Luke 2:25, Acts 2:5, and Acts 8:2. What makes a person devout? Really dig deep here, do some research.

_____
_____
_____
_____
_____
_____
_____
_____

The Gleaner, state paper, church bulletin

I use these periodicals in conjunction with my prayer journal. As I am reading my *Gleaner* (not during my personal quiet time), I underline prayer requests in the articles from the missionaries. In my quiet time I place these requests on appropriate pages in my journal. Then I turn *The Gleaner* to the monthly prayer calendar and use it every day. During the "Fifty Days of Prayer and Giving" the missions devotional guide is also in my tool basket. I use my state paper, *The Baptist Trumpet,* and my church bulletin in the same way I use *The Gleaner.* The more informed you are, the more concerned you are.

❏ Yes ❏ No Do you read *The Gleaner*?
❏ Yes ❏ No Do you read your state paper?
❏ Yes ❏ No Do you read your church bulletin?

How can you personally make better use of these three pieces of material?

_____
_____

How do these three pieces of material relate to the word *missionary* in our name Women's Missionary Auxiliary?

_____
_____
_____
_____

Patsy Campbell

Pens, pencils, erasers, highlighters

Let me say just a word about these tools. Put them in a plastic bag and have an ample supply on hand for use. Remember, Satan will do anything to hinder your time with God. Don't let useless interruptions happen when a little preparation can prevent them. Be able to say, "Get thee behind me, Satan, I've been proactive and you don't get the victory in my prayer life."

Other items

As you get deeper and deeper into your quiet time, you get better and better at it. You will become more and more comfortable with the tools and use them with ease. You may want to add a concordance, handbook, Greek lexicon, or perhaps an atlas. You may decide to remove some tools you don't use. Just keep working on your tool basket. It's full now, but will change from time to time. One more reminder, ladies — decently and in order.

Evaluate your persistence as you begin to practice a personal quiet time. After the first two weeks of your personal quiet time, write your thoughts here about your experience. How have you changed?

_____
_____
_____
_____
_____
_____
_____

After two more weeks, write your thoughts here. How do you now feel about abiding in the Lord?

_____
_____
_____
_____
_____
_____
_____

Pray, Work, Win!

After another month, write your thoughts here. Record your thoughts about the faithfulness of God.

_____

_____

_____

_____

_____

After three months, write your thoughts here. Reflect on your personal growth.

_____

_____

_____

_____

_____

Please take these final exercises seriously. Do them periodically as a checkup on how you are doing. When you have reached the first anniversary of beginning your daily time with God, take out your jotting journal and record your thoughts on your joys, sorrows, victories, defeats, lessons, and growth. Particularly answer the question: "How do you feel about prayer now?" If you have time drop me a note, I would love to have you share with me.

Chapter 2

Get Real

When praying to your heavenly Father, remember to Whom you are speaking — the God of heaven; the Creator Who is omnipotent, omniscient, and omnipresent; your personal Savior; your sovereign Lord.

Stop now and express in your own words the answer to the question "Who is God?"

_____

_____

_____

_____

_____

Let me suggest that you get real with God in two ways: Know God; Know Yourself. This dialogue will be between just you and God. You need to get to know each other well.

Know God

I want to suggest two studies for your quiet time: *The Names of God* (Thomas Nelson Publishers) and *The Attributes of God* by A. W. Tozer.

You can use the concordance in your Bible to study the names of God, or you can buy a book on the subject. *The Names of God* listed above and *To Know Him by Name* by Kay Arthur are two good sources.

One day in my quiet time, I was using my hymnal and just opened it to "A Mighty Fortress Is Our God." As I was praying the first verse of this hymn, I thought of my ongoing study on the names of God. *Fortress* is a name for God and He has truly been a fortress for me. I had not intended to study a name of God that day, but felt led to do so. I found scripture references for fortress and did some journaling. That study has been such a blessing to me that I now have about thirty names for God and have no idea where or when it will end. I know each name I study helps me to know God more deeply and He becomes much more real in my praying. This study has been going for several years. Share with me in the word *fortress*.

Define *fortress*:

_____

_____

Pray, Work, Win!

Find two or more scriptures concerning fortress and write them here.

_____

_____

_____

_____

Look up the hymn "A Mighty Fortress Is Our God." Read, sing, or pray the verses to God. Write down the phrase that means the most to you and tell why.

_____

_____

_____

_____

Think of one or more times in your life when God has really been a fortress for you. List those times here.

_____

_____

_____

_____

_____

_____

To do the work on fortress may take you more than one quiet time; it may even take several.

Another example is *jealous*. As I was preparing one of the Sunday School lessons in Ezekiel during the spring quarter 2002, I referenced the scripture Exodus 34:14, *"For thou shalt worship no other god: for the LORD, whose name is Jealous, is a jealous God."* As of this writing, I have not done this name of God yet, but I have added it to my list and one day soon it will be my study topic in my personal quiet time.

Find another name for God that is very meaningful to you. Work through this name in the same way you did *Fortress*.

The name of God I choose for study is _____.

Patsy Campbell

Now let us trace God's name in the Bible from the very first reference. Look up Genesis 1:1 and write it here.

_____

_____

_____

Using the notes in your own Bible, write what you found that name to be and what it means.

_____

_____

_____

Is this name used in singular or plural? _____
What is the significance of this discovery?

_____

_____

As I studied the names of God I used my Scofield King James Version Bible. For my study of the attributes of God, I just used my concordance. In my journal, I made a page entitled "Attributes of God," and on this particular page listed each attribute. In my study time I journal whatever God gives to me on each of these attributes. One day while doing my attributes study the word *awesome* just jumped up at me, so I knew this was the attribute to study today.

Deuteronomy 7:21 and 10:17 use the word *terrible* to describe God. Write those two verses below.

_____

_____

_____

_____

_____

_____

What does the word *terrible* mean as a description of God?

_____

_____

_____

Pray, Work, Win!

Define *awesome*.

_____

_____

Compare your definition for *awesome* and the use of the word *terrible* in these two verses.

_____

_____

_____

Recall a time in your life when you needed an awesome God. How did God meet your need at the time?

_____

_____

_____

_____

_____

Later in the day, I just kept thinking of awesome and looked up the chorus "Our God Is an Awesome God." Right then I put that chorus book in my tool basket to use in my quiet time the next day.

I do hope you begin to see how study subjects develop. As God leads and directs your quiet time, He also deepens your trust and fellowship. As you keep studying God in all His aspects (which by the way is a study you will never exhaust) you will get more real in your praying.

One last study suggestion on the names of God is to go to the Gospel of John and find the names of God listed in this book. Write the names down, give the scripture where you found it, and write what this name means to you personally.

Let me get you started.

1. The Word — John 1:1

_____

_____

_____

_____

_____

2. Lamb of God who takes away the sin of the world — John 1:29, 35

_____

_____

_____

_____

_____

_____

3. Bread of Life — John 6:35

_____

_____

_____

_____

_____

_____

Continue this exercise throughout the book of John. Record your findings in your journal.

Know yourself

Now, let's move to knowing yourself. Psalm 139:14 says, *"I will praise thee; for I am fearfully and wonderfully made."* We are made by God and we are very intricate. When we think of who we are, many words come to mind. Study each word in the list below. Define it, describe how it relates to you, and find a scripture to go with each word.

1. Body

_____

_____

_____

_____

_____

_____

2. Soul

3. Spirit

4. Mind

5. Emotion

6. Will

7. Affections

Pray, Work, Win!

8. Desires

_____
_____
_____
_____
_____
_____

Let's now consider personality. For your work on this study, I want to suggest you work through chapters 4 and 5 of the book *In His Presents* by Judy Wallace.

Are you predominately …

❑ The popular Sanguine
❑ The powerful Choleric
❑ The perfect Melancholy
❑ The peaceful Phlegmatic

Place the number 1 by your predominant personality and the number 2 by your next strongest personality. Later in this chapter, I will ask you to write about this exercise.

Let's consider your spiritual gifts. Do an inventory to find your gifts. Many churches have done this in recent years and you may know your primary and secondary gifts already. It would be beneficial to do an inventory just to be current. You can get an inventory at a bookstore, from your pastor, or use the one in Judy Wallace's book *In His Presents*. There are several good inventories and whichever one you choose will show you your gifts.

Spiritual gifts are listed here. Define each one and write a scripture concerning that gift.

1. Prophet

_____
_____
_____
_____
_____

2. Evangelist

3. Teacher

4. Exhortation

5. Wisdom

6. Knowledge

7. Helps (Taking care of things)

8. Serving

9. Leadership

10. Administration

11. Giving

12. Mercy

13. Discernment

Pray, Work, Win!

14. Faith

_____
_____
_____
_____
_____
_____

My Gifts:
  Primary _____
  Secondary _____

❏ Yes ❏ No   Were you surprised by your primary gift?

What new discovery did you make about your gifts?

_____
_____
_____

❏ Yes ❏ No   Was there one or more gifts you would like to have, but found them to be low in your scoring on the inventory?

What are these gifts?

_____

It may take time to complete this section. When you have completed it, you are ready to do some journaling on the subject of "Who I Am and Who I Can Be." Go back and read what you wrote about who you are on each of the ten words you researched. Read what you have written about spiritual gifts. Write whatever the Lord leads you to write and be as honest as you possibly can. Remember, God already knows you better than you know yourself. You must discover who you are right now; then you need to look at who you can be, who you want to be, and most importantly of all, who God wants you to be.

Stop just now and pray for God to lead you in this essay!

Write this essay in your journal. It will possibly take several pages. Title it: "Who I Am and Who I Can Be!"

Here is an extended assignment for you to work. As you continue to know God better and know more about yourself, write one or two sentences each week for three months describing how this exercise has improved your prayer life. (Enter the date in the first short blank and the sentences after each week number.)

_____ 1. _____
_____

_____ 2. _____
_____

_____ 3. _____
_____

_____ 4. _____
_____

_____ 5. _____
_____

_____ 6. _____
_____

_____ 7. _____
_____

_____ 8. _____
_____

_____ 9. _____
_____

_____ 10. _____
_____

_____ 11. _____
_____

_____ 12. _____
_____

Pray, Work, Win!

This next assignment will come *one year later*. One year after the last date you wrote at number 12, do this exercise again.

I really want you to have a strong daily quiet time, prayer time, and growing time. Hang in there with me and you will just be amazed at what God will do in your life.

Remember, this is a journey of a lifetime, not just some weekend outings or overnight stopovers. Please read Ephesians 3:19-20, *"To know the love of Christ, which passeth knowledge, that ye might be filled with all the fulness of God. Now unto him that is able to do exceeding abundantly above all that we ask or think, according to the power that worketh in us."* You may want to pray these verses to God just now.

Chapter 3

Affirm God

How do we affirm God? Let's look at the word *affirm*. It means "to state with confidence, to assert positively." Some other words that will amplify the word *affirm* are: assert, profess, maintain, testify, certify, emphasize, stress, and enforce. One definition I really like is "insist upon." In every way I know how, with every fiber of my being, I want to affirm God. I insist upon the fact that God *is*. Genesis 1:1 says, *"In the beginning God created the heaven and the earth."*

Search for and record scriptures that allow you to affirm the following truths about God.

I insist upon the fact that God always was and always will be.

(Scripture) _____

_____

I insist upon the fact that God saved me, and that only God could do that.

(Scripture) _____

_____

I insist that beyond saving grace, God provides me daily with keeping grace for my every need.

(Scripture) _____

_____

I insist upon the fact that even at this moment God is preparing my mansion.

(Scripture) _____

_____

I do affirm God and praise God. He always affirms me. He never lets me down, He always knows and accepts me as His child.

(Scripture) _____

_____

Write your own statement to affirm God.

_____

_____

Pray, Work, Win!

Our prayer life gives us great opportunities to affirm God. In this chapter I want to examine several elements of our praying that allow us to affirm truths about God. First, I want to link three elements together: praise, adoration, and thanksgiving. If you will begin your prayer time with these elements you will indeed avoid the laundry list syndrome.

Don't you like to be loved? Doesn't it just give you a warm feeling for someone to say, "I love You"? Isn't it especially rewarding for someone close to tell you this? It shows you are not being taken for granted by spouse, child, family, or close friends. Well, God loves you and loves to be loved by you.

We don't often think about how God feels when we miss our time with Him. We know it affects us negatively when we miss daily time with God, but God misses us too. Please write a short comment on how God feels if we don't commune with Him in prayer.

_____

_____

_____

Adore means "to have deep love for, esteem, reverence, and admire." We must adore God and honor Him with our private and public worship. *Praise* means "to express approval, to glorify." *Thanksgiving* is expressing gratitude, gratitude to God for all His bounty and blessings. Beginning with our salvation, we have so much to thank God for that we can never spend too much time in being thankful.

Let's do a little work with these elements. Find a scripture that you really like for *each* of these three elements. Write the scriptures here and then tell why you like this scripture.

Love/Adore

_____

_____

_____

_____

_____

_____

_____

_____

Praise

_____
_____
_____
_____
_____
_____
_____
_____

Thanksgiving

_____
_____
_____
_____
_____

Make a journal entry now about how you think beginning with these three elements will change your prayer life. Discuss your ideas in your WMA or ladies meeting.

Confession is really important in affirming God. Confession says, "I agree with You, Lord. I have sinned, and I do need to be forgiven. I know You are the *only* One Who can forgive."

These three elements — praise, adoration, and thanksgiving — will truly help with confession. Confession is hard because it is difficult to be wrong or admit fault. We tend to want to say "Forgive my sins," but what we really need to do is be specific with God about our sins. We really need to talk to God about our sins, repent, and ask God to show us how He wants us to change. Confession really teaches us so much about ourselves. It doesn't teach God anything. He already knows us better than we do. *Confession* means "to admit fault or debt, to own the personal responsibility for wrongdoing." *Responsible* means "to be reliable or trustworthy."

Please write 1 John 1:9 here.

_____
_____

Pray, Work, Win!

Please write Proverbs 28:13 here.

_____
_____

How do these two verses relate to you personally?

_____
_____
_____
_____

❏ Yes ❏ No Do you have unconfessed sins in your life?

If the answer is yes, many things in your Christian life are in jeopardy. Your fellowship, your worship, and your service are three important areas that will be affected.

Please comment on how you will change your prayer life with regard to confession.

_____
_____
_____

The next elements of our prayer lives that I would link together are silence, listening, and meditation. Please remember that prayer is a conversation or dialogue. We are talking to God, and God is talking to us. Ask yourself, "When I am praying, do I breathe? Do I pause and give God His turn in our conversation?"

Do you ever feel God saying, "Child, let Me get a word in!" Do you begin, talk pretty rapidly, then get up and go about your business? Do you find that you have very little peace or satisfaction from praying?

Silence means "the absence of noise, stillness, muteness." Psalm 46:10 reads, *"Be still, and know that I am God."*

Write 1 Kings 19:12 here.

_____
_____

Listen means "to give attention to something in order to hear it; to give heed, to follow advice." You may be wondering what you are listening for. God is not going to speak audibly as He did to Moses in the burning bush. When you are practicing silence with the expectation of hearing from God, you will hear

Him. Perhaps a scripture will come to you. Perhaps someone will call and say just what you need to hear, or perhaps something in a sermon will especially speak to your heart. God has many ways to speak if you will only listen.

Write Psalm 85:8 here and what it means for you.

_____
_____
_____
_____
_____

List some ways God has spoken to you.

_____
_____
_____
_____
_____

Meditation means "to quietly consider something carefully." Please write 1 Timothy 4:15 here and what it teaches you.

_____
_____
_____
_____
_____

The next two prayer elements are asking and interceding. These elements are vastly different. *Ask* means "to inquire, to make a request, to ask for help." *Intercede* means "to act as a go-between, to beg or plead in behalf of another to the point of sacrifice." Intercession is bold and daring. When we intercede, we are determined, and we don't give up until an answer is received. Christians who have become true intercessors have matured in their prayer lives. They feel an inescapable responsibility to pray for others, and they feel prayer is a distinct privilege.

Pray, Work, Win!

Write 1 Timothy 2:1.

_____

_____

What is the significance in this verse of the word *all*?

_____

_____

_____

How does this verse relate to praying for Muslims and others with whom we do not agree?

_____

_____

_____

How does anger block intercession?

_____

_____

_____

Write Ephesians 6:18 and what it teaches you.

_____

_____

_____

_____

_____

❏ Yes ❏ No Do you consider yourself a true intercessor?

How could you become an intercessor?

_____

_____

_____

If you believe that salvation is *the* only way for any person to get on the right track, why is true intercession for salvation so important?

_____

_____

Praying scripture is an element that we often overlook in our praying. If you go to any Christian bookstore, you will discover an explosion of books on praying scripture. You may want to get a book on this subject and put it in your prayer basket to use in your daily quiet time. The best way to pray scripture is to do it consistently. I previously asked you to write a prayer from your life verses. Now, here are some specific scriptures to pray to God. Write out a prayer for each verse. Be personal, specific, and actually pray aloud to God what you have written. Please do this exercise in your journal as I did not leave space here. Here are the scripture references: Psalm 23; Philippians 4:13; Matthew 5:6; Job 5:17; Galatians 5:22-23.

Praying scripture can become a significant part of your prayer life. This exercise is not just a space filler. I really want you to practice praying God's Word to Him in your own words. I suggest now that you choose five more scriptures that God gives you and pray them to God. The more you pray scripture, the easier it is and the more you learn from it. By the time you write prayers for the five scriptures I gave you and the five scriptures God led you to use, you will begin to be comfortable with praying scripture. This exercise is for your benefit, so take as long as you need, even if it takes weeks.

We began with the element of praise and will end with the element of praise. This takes your praying full circle and leaves no loose ends.

After completing this section on affirming God, write a summary of your thoughts.

_____

_____

_____

_____

_____

_____

_____

_____

_____

Pray, Work, Win!

Chapter 4

Yield

The triangular yield sign is familiar to every driver. When coming to the yield sign, the driver must remember that she does not have the right of way. She must give that right of way to approaching traffic. *Yield* means "to surrender to another." Believers must give God the right of way in their lives.

It is easy to talk about yielding. Yielding is really an easy concept to understand with the head, but it is a really hard thing to put into practice in life. Putting the principle into practice means surrendering our hearts, but we are proud and vain. We are strong willed, and we do not want anyone else running our lives or telling us what to do. Yielding to God is an area in our lives that requires much concentration and work. The only way to successfully yield to the Lord is through prayer.

There are two scriptures I would like for you to consider. The first is 2 Chronicles 30:8. Write it here.

_____

_____

_____

The next verse is Romans 6:13. Write it here.

_____

_____

_____

Describe your desire to be yielded to God.

_____

_____

_____

_____

Pray, Work, Win!

Think of three things you could do in your life to help you yield to God and list them in this space.

1. _____

_____

2. _____

_____

3. _____

_____

Take time right now to pray and ask God to help you have a life that is truly yielded to your heavenly Father.

In the next section of the book we will study the believer's work. I would like you to comment here about how being yielded *to* God affects your work *for* God.

_____

_____

_____

_____

_____

_____

_____

_____

Section Two — Work
Willing
Organized
Risking
Kinds

Not saved? Can't pray.

Saved, don't pray? Won't work.

Saved, strong daily prayer commitment? Ready to do God's work, God's way.

These steps are like rungs in a ladder. Salvation is the first rung. Daily quiet time with our heavenly Father in prayer is the second rung of our climb. Now, the third rung is to find the work God has for us to do and be meaningfully engaged in it. Salvation puts us in the position to pray, and it puts us in the position to work for God in the ministry He has called us to do. Many times we look at salvation simply as the act which keeps us from going to hell, and it certainly does that, but God wants more for us. He wants our lives to bring honor and glory to Him.

Write 2 Timothy 2:21 here and then record your thoughts on what this verse teaches you about work.

_____

_____

_____

_____

_____

_____

Pray, Work, Win!

Chapter 5

Willing

God calls believers to follow His will in His way. Christians must choose whether they are willing to obey. Many times they are willing to do the work of God if they get to choose what they want to do. The truth is that God does the choosing and His children do the obeying.

Can you obey?

Write Philippians 4:13 here and share how this verse impacts your life.

___

___

___

___

___

What happens to our working for God if we omit *"through Christ"* from this verse?

___

___

Define the words *ability* and *availability*.

Ability means ___

___

Availability means ___

___

Record your thoughts about how these two words play a part in your work for God.

___

___

___

Pray, Work, Win!

Where do we get our strength for God's work?

_____

_____

Give an example of some work in your life you could not have done except that the Lord did it through you.

_____

_____

_____

_____

_____

Give an example of a work you tried that failed. Why did it fail?

_____

_____

_____

_____

_____

What is significant about the phrase *channel of blessing* as it relates to God's work?

_____

_____

_____

Must you obey?

Is Matthew 5:16 a command or a suggestion? Explain your answer.

_____

_____

_____

_____

_____

Write Luke 2:49 here.

_____

_____

Who is speaking? _____

Was He God's Son? _____

Are you a child of God? _____

Do *you* have your Father's work that you must do? Explain.

_____

_____

_____

Write Matthew 21:28 here.

_____

_____

How are obedience and work related?

_____

_____

Write 2 Thessalonians 3:10 here.

_____

_____

Discuss this verse from a spiritual perspective. Be sure to comment on work, fellowship, and blessing.

_____

_____

_____

_____

_____

_____

_____

Pray, Work, Win!

Will you obey?

You can obey because God will enable you to obey. You must obey because God has commanded it for His glory. Now, most importantly, will you obey? *Will you?* is the most important of the trilogy. Can you? Must you? Will you?

Why is this question the most important? Because it is the action piece. It is the *getting it done* piece. It is the accomplishment, the finished product. If I say I can and don't; if I say I must and won't, the work is not done. If I say I will and *do*, the kingdom work moves forward. It causes growth. It causes deeper fellowship. It causes deeper commitment, and it causes more work to be done.

Use your personal journal to write about *I will* as it relates to your personal work for God.

_____

_____

_____

_____

Find one or two scriptures about willingness. Write them here.

_____

_____

_____

_____

_____

_____

Now pray them to God. (Write those verses in your own words as a prayer.)

_____

_____

_____

_____

_____

I want you to spend some time in studying Ephesians 4 and 5:1-17. This passage is about the believer's walk and the believer's service. First, read through the entire section. Then take as long as you need to be thorough with this passage.

What does it mean to be a prisoner of the Lord (4:1)?

_____

_____

_____

How does one walk worthy (4:1)?

_____

_____

_____

List the seven unities (4:4-5). 1. _____

2. _____ 3. _____ 4. _____

5. _____ 6. _____ 7. _____

Why are these unities significant?

_____

_____

_____

How does Ephesians 4:7-8 support the fact that all of us who are saved have work(s) to do?

_____

_____

_____

_____

Why do we work for the Lord (4:12)?

_____

_____

_____

Pray, Work, Win!

Discuss what it means to think with a new mind (4:17-24).

_____
_____
_____
_____
_____
_____

Why is the indwelling of the Holy Spirit important to our work for God (4:30-32)?

_____
_____
_____
_____

We should be _____ of _____ as _____ _____ (Ephesians 5:1).

Why is following as a child important to our work?

_____
_____

Discuss Ephesians 5:8.

_____
_____

How do we redeem time by our works for God (5:16).

_____
_____
_____

Ephesians 5:17 reminds us not to be unwise, but to understand the will of the Lord. How can you understand the will of the Lord for your life?

_____

_____

_____

_____

_____

What is the correlation between your passion to be in the center of God's will in your life and your work for the Lord?

_____

_____

_____

_____

_____

_____

_____

Pray, Work, Win!

Chapter 6

Organized

First Corinthians 14:40 says, *"Let all things be done decently and in order."* Remember those helpers; they'll be our friends.

What does this verse imply about efficiency?

_____

_____

What does this verse imply about wasting time?

_____

_____

What does this verse imply about personal frustration?

_____

_____

Comment on the significance of the word *all* in this verse.

_____

_____

Please recall a time when lack of organization robbed you of a victory in your work for the Lord. Write about the incident here.

_____

_____

_____

_____

_____

_____

_____

I want you to do an acrostic for the word *organized*. Get your dictionary and go through each letter to find a word that speaks to you. I have done the first

Pray, Work, Win!

three. There are no wrong answers; this is just what God lays on your heart, and I'm sure everyone's acrostic will be different.

Open: Be open-minded and share ideas about organizing your life. After brainstorming, make a plan. Then arrange the steps in order to accomplish the task.

R eady: Don't begin until you are sure God is ready. After much prayer and preparation, let God set your startup time.

G od: Let God be at the beginning, in the middle, and at the end of every work you do for Him. If you put God first, pride will not slip in so easily.

A _____

_____

_____

N _____

_____

_____

I _____

_____

_____

Z _____

_____

_____

E _____

_____

_____

D _____

_____

_____

Patsy Campbell

Now that your acrostic is complete, read back over it and make an overall comment here.

_____
_____
_____
_____
_____
_____
_____

I cannot say enough about the importance of organization in doing God's work. We have so many important things to fit into our daily schedules. We have to take care of household chores and prepare meals. Our jobs claim a significant part of each day. If we are not organized, the Lord's work will definitely get placed on the back burner.

We need to get in the habit of organizing every part of our lives in concert. Our job can't be put in one compartment, our family in another, or our work for God in another. We should seek a definite flow to the whole twenty-four hours.

Three words are important here: flight, fight, flow. Without good organization, you will run away. You'll have a daily flight plan, and your percentage of accomplishment will be very low. The devil will get the victory in your life. God will not be honored, neither will you be a winner. Or, you will put up your dukes to fight and come out of your corner swinging with your anger quotient zooming. The people in your household will not be happy campers. So a harum-scarum lifestyle robs your calm and fosters frustration instead. The devil wins again. This fight posture can even end in divorce, and the devil has stolen your family.

You can, on the other hand, organize your day with all areas accounted for and in order. You will make necessary adjustments as the need arises, but for the most part you will follow your original plan. The devil is rousted and you win.

Is flow the panacea for every problem? Of course not, but it sure beats flight and fight. Organizing your life to flow will steadily increase the degree of success in your life. This plan of organization will insure that your work for God gets done because it is one aspect of your life that will logically fit into your daily twenty-four hours.

Pray, Work, Win!

List in order the steps you feel that you need to take to become better organized.

_____

_____

_____

_____

_____

_____

_____

_____

_____

_____

Chapter 7

Risk

Risk is about trusting God and not self. It is believing God is Who He says He is. Risk is about believing we are nothing — it's all God. Risk is seeing the victory before beginning the task — getting a vision of success. Risk is about believing beyond the shadow of a doubt that when God calls, He equips.

God wants you to be a winner. He loved you, saved you, and He has called you to work in His field. God sees you as a winner. You must see yourself the same way. If you are not normally a risk taker, you will have some major work to do here.

Pray

Really pray about God's plan for your life. What work has God given you? What does God want you to risk? God does not want you to remain on the same level day after day. He has more for you. He wants growth. He wants both greater quantity and better quality.

Commit

Commit yourself to God. He must come before anything else in your life. Don't let anyone or anything be the excuse you use for not serving God.

What excuses are you using to avoid serving God?

_____

_____

_____

_____

Why is it dangerous to seek excuses?

_____

_____

Define *commitment*.

_____

_____

Pray, Work, Win!

How does commitment relate to risk, work, completion, and victory?

_____

_____

_____

_____

Risk

Begin to risk. Stop saying no to things you don't believe you can do. Remember, God does the work, and you are His channel. At first, take a small risk. Do you know how to eat an elephant? One small bite at a time. Taking small steps will build your risk quotient. First, take a small step, and then experience victory. Don't be mistaken. You will be victorious because God is Who He says He is, and victory is His plan for you. Small victories will prepare you to take larger risks until your trust in God has built to such a level that you just automatically take risks for Him.

Write Ephesians 2:8-10 here.

_____

_____

_____

_____

_____

Share your thoughts on the sufficiency and efficiency of God's grace.

_____

_____

_____

Why should we work for God (2:10)?

_____

_____

_____

Give all the credit to God. The pronoun *I* should be absent from your work for God. *He* should be present in your work for Him.

Write 1 Corinthians 6:20 here.

_____

_____

_____

_____

What price did God pay to purchase your life?

_____

_____

Because of this price, your work should:

_____

Write Ephesians 4:12 here.

_____

_____

_____

According to this verse, what else should we do besides glorify God?

_____

_____

Define *edify*.

_____

_____

What are some positive effects of edifying?

_____

_____

_____

_____

_____

_____

Pray, Work, Win!

What are some negative effects of criticizing?

How are *you* glorifying God and edifying His church?

Risk-takers are light spreaders. Write Matthew 5:14-16.

We are the _____ of the _____. Why is this important?

❑ Yes ❑ No Are you under a bushel?
If you answered yes, how can you come out?

_____

_____

_____

_____

_____

Why must we shine our lights (Matthew 5:16)?

1. _____

_____

2. _____

_____

Remember, our good works are seen by other people, but if our hearts and our attitudes are right, it is our Father in heaven who gets the glory.
Do you want to be a risk taker for God?
What are your fears about this?

_____

_____

_____

_____

What are some changes you will have to make in your life?

_____

_____

_____

_____

_____

_____

Pray, Work, Win!

What do you feel God is calling you to risk right now for Him?

_____
_____
_____
_____

How will you measure your success?

_____
_____
_____
_____
_____
_____

Chapter 8

Kinds

I want you to list all the kinds of work you can think of to do for God. No task is too small or too large. Just let your mind be creative. Ask friends to help with your list. Ask your pastor if there are jobs or ministries your church needs. Brainstorm for items to add to your list in a WMA or ladies ministry meeting.

Below I've included one hundred spaces for you to write ideas. Make this an ongoing list to which you keep adding tasks. If you can see the need and the possibility of accomplishment, you will have a much greater potential to start the work. This list should become a work in progress. If you never even think of a certain job, you will never do it. I have given a few jobs to start your list.

Kinds of work for God

1. Prayer warrior
2. Make bulletin boards with photos and church news for nursing home patients and shut-ins. Change them regularly.
3. Committee member
4. Nursery coordinator or helper
5. Choir member; play an instrument
6. Teacher; assistant
7. Carry food when needed
8. Fall carnival for neighborhood
9. Intercessory prayer ministry
10. Craft and supply room for church-wide use
11. Equip and maintain a prayer room
12. Coordinator for BMMI in your church
13. Form an active mission committee
14. Form a weekly prayer group to pray for our missionaries
15. Work in church visitation
16. Attend and work in the local association and WMA
17. Attend and work in the state association and WMA
18. Attend and work in the national association and WMA
19. Be involved in fund raising for projects
20. Visit shut-ins on a regular basis
21. Visit nursing home patients regularly

Pray, Work, Win!

22. Hospital visitation ministry
23. Work in the church library
24. Serve as class officer
25. Go on a mission trip
26. Do volunteer work for the BMAA
27. Have a ministry using banners in your church
28. Maintain a birthday file on church family; send cards
29. Work with drama ministry
30. Help youth form a praise band
31. _____
32. _____
33. _____
34. _____
35. _____
36. _____
37. _____
38. _____
39. _____
40. _____
41. _____
42. _____
43. _____
44. _____
45. _____
46. _____
47. _____
48. _____
49. _____
50. _____

51. _____
52. _____
53. _____
54. _____
55. _____
56. _____
57. _____
58. _____
59. _____
60. _____
61. _____
62. _____
63. _____
64. _____
65. _____
66. _____
67. _____
68. _____
69. _____
70. _____
71. _____
72. _____
73. _____
74. _____
75. _____
76. _____

77. _____
78. _____
79. _____
80. _____
81. _____
82. _____
83. _____
84. _____
85. _____
86. _____
87. _____
88. _____
89. _____
90. _____
91. _____
92. _____
93. _____
94. _____
95. _____
96. _____
97. _____
98. _____
99. _____
100. _____

I would be thrilled for you to send me a copy of your list to help me with new ideas for service. I would love to talk with you about any ideas I have listed to help you get started. The first step is always the hardest. Don't forget to *risk*!

Go over your list now and review how you are currently involved in each service. Be sure God has called you to each one. Comment on the importance of God's direction in this evaluation.

_____

_____

_____

_____

List those areas you feel you need to add to your work and explain why.

_____

_____

_____

_____

List those areas in which you are currently involved that you feel need to be eliminated and explain why.

_____

_____

_____

_____

_____

Remember, your work involves many choices. You can't do everything. God has not called you to everything. You must decide what is *good, better,* or *best*. All God's work is necessary and good, but you must find God's work that He has especially for you. How can you choose your special areas of service?

_____

_____

_____

_____

Pray, Work, Win!

List some ministries where your church should be involved, but it is not at this time.

_____

_____

_____

_____

List some ways you might help in this effort.

_____

_____

_____

_____

Organization is so important to any work you undertake. You must take certain steps — in order — to have success. I want to share a simple plan with you so you get the idea. With this type of plan you can do any project large or small. It's really a road map to keep you on the right path. Consider a tract ministry as an example.

To begin, you must pray constantly for the ministry. Then, to initiate the ministry you must plan clearly in several different areas.

Personnel resources. Choose a person to coordinate the ministry. Clearly explain the responsibilities of the task which include (1) Ordering tracts, (2) Filling tract racks, (3) Researching the availability of tracts and polling for suggestions, (4) Publicizing the ministry, (5) Educating members about how to use the tracts.

Procedure. (1) Place tract racks in at least two prominent places in church. (2) Keep racks fully stocked. (3) Initiate plans to train people how to use tracts.

Publicize. (1) Through the church bulletin encourage all members to use tracts. Place this reminder in the bulletin once every quarter. (2) Go into each Sunday School class and speak briefly about the tract ministry. (3) At least twice a year have a different church member share a success story in the morning worship service.

Educate. (1) Demonstrate to members that they can leave tracts *everywhere* they go: doctors' offices, restaurants, library, grocery, cleaners, etc. (2) Suggest that members enclose a tract in each piece of mail they send. (3) Twice a year pass out a list of suggestions on ways to use the tracts.

You can see that this ministry takes a lot of work. You can't just begin it and then leave it. This principle is true of all ministries. They must be worked. If you were the coordinator of the tract ministry, you couldn't be involved in too many other ministries that also took a lot of time. Organization, prayer, and constantly working the ministry insure success.

Now, I want you to practice writing an organization plan. This is simply choosing a ministry and composing an orderly list of the steps to success. Choose a ministry in which you are currently involved or one you wish to begin.

Ministry organization plan

Name of ministry: _____

Steps to success. List the steps in order and number each step.

_____
_____
_____
_____
_____
_____
_____
_____
_____
_____
_____
_____
_____
_____
_____
_____
_____
_____

At one of your WMA or ladies ministry meetings spend some time sharing these plans with each other.

Pray, Work, Win!

What did you learn about organization?

_____
_____
_____
_____

What did you learn about working your plan year after year?

_____
_____
_____
_____
_____

Why will the plan need to be updated on a regular basis?

_____
_____
_____
_____

Why do you think many things get started, go for a time, and then end?

_____
_____
_____
_____

Do you think this is God's way of doing business? Why?

___

Write John 9:4-5 here.

___

Comment on these two verses as they relate to your work for the Lord.

___

The third and final section of this study is on winning. How are *work* and *winning* related?

___

Pray, Work, Win!

Section Three — Win
Wise
It's All About You, Lord
Never Give Up

Let's be really hard-down honest. We like to be winners! Practice the guidelines given and you will be a winner. Winning is the top rung on that ladder we talked about in section 2. The first step is salvation followed by prayer and daily quiet time. Next comes the actual work. Finally you *will* win because God promised to reward faithful service. Claim God's promise!

Write 1 Corinthians 4:2 here. What does this verse teach you?

_____

_____

_____

_____

_____

Choose three of your favorite Bible characters who really demonstrated their faithfulness to God. Write a paragraph concerning each one and include scripture references which show the character's faithfulness.
First character:

_____

_____

_____

_____

_____

_____

_____

_____

_____

_____

Pray, Work, Win!

Second character:

Third character:

Now, write a paragraph about your faithfulness. Be honest!

_____
_____
_____
_____
_____
_____
_____
_____
_____
_____
_____
_____

Discuss these paragraphs in your WMA or ladies ministry meeting.

Pray, Work, Win!

Chapter 9

Wise

Many scriptures focus on wisdom and being wise. The only verse I want to share here is Proverbs 11:30. Write the verse here.

_____

_____

_____

Soul winning is the *best* work.
Soul winning gives us the victory in witnessing.
Soul winning is so many times neglected.
Soul winning adds precious souls to God's family.
Soul winning is for every Christian.

If you want to *win* for God, be a soul winner. Comment on your work as a soul winner.

_____

_____

_____

_____

_____

What blocks your efforts at witnessing?

_____

_____

_____

_____

_____

_____

_____

Pray, Work, Win!

What can you do to overcome these blocks?

_____

_____

_____

_____

_____

_____

When will you begin?

_____

How is your church involved in regular, active, organized soul-winning?

_____

_____

_____

_____

_____

How does seeing souls saved, baptized, and regularly added to the church deepen the worship of that church?

_____

_____

_____

_____

_____

_____

Why do you think we are not more committed to soul winning?

_____
_____
_____
_____
_____
_____

The subject of winning often prompts us to think about the prize of our victory. The reward of Christian service will be a crown. Write 2 Timothy 4:7-8 here.

_____
_____
_____
_____
_____
_____
_____
_____

Why do you receive a crown (4:7)?

_____
_____
_____

Who will give the crown (4:8? _____

When will it be given (4:8)? _____

Pray, Work, Win!

Is salvation a reward? ❏ Yes ❏ No Give scripture.

_____
_____
_____
_____

Is a crown a reward? ❏ Yes ❏ No Explain and give scripture.

_____
_____
_____
_____
_____

What are you going to do with your crown?

_____
_____
_____

Why (Revelation 4:11)?

_____
_____
_____
_____

Chapter 10

It's All About You, Lord

Our study now arrives at the point of getting ourselves *totally* out of the way. Christian service *is* all about the Lord. It is not our work; it's His work for which we are privileged to be His channels. Let's look at some examples of His work.
- From 32,000 to 300.
- Don't cut my hair.
- I'll always be faithful and own your name.
- Will the wall fall?

The first example comes from Judges 7:1-25.

Who is God's man in this passage? _____

Who is his enemy? _____

What do you learn about pride from Judges 7:2?

_____
_____
_____
_____

How was the first group of Israelite soldiers eliminated?

_____
_____

How many remained? _____

How was the second group of soldiers eliminated?

_____
_____
_____

How many remained? _____

What is significant about Judges 7:9?

_____
_____

93

Pray, Work, Win!

How do you know the Midianites were a huge army (7:12)?
_____
_____

What was the dream that Gideon overheard a man telling (7:13)?
_____
_____

How do you know Gideon totally trusted in God and not in himself (7:15)?
_____
_____
_____

What were their weapons of war?
1.
2.
3.

Who drew up the battle plan? ❑ Gideon ❑ God

Verse 20 is significant because of the phrase, *"The sword of the LORD, and of Gideon."* It's all about You, Lord, and You just let me be a part of Your great work.

The second example from our list comes from Judges 13-16.

Who is God's man in this passage? _____

Who are the Nazarites?
_____
_____

What did the angel tell Samson's mother in the last part of Judges 13:5?
_____
_____
_____

How do we learn the angels accept no credit, but give it all to God (13:16)?

_____

_____

How do we know God's hand is guiding Samson (13:24-25)?

_____

_____

_____

What is Samson's riddle (14:14)?

_____

_____

_____

What does it mean (14:18)?

_____

_____

How was the riddle discovered (14:18)?

_____

_____

What happened to the crops of the Philistines (15:4-5)?

_____

_____

_____

_____

Pray, Work, Win!

How do we know God had not forsaken Samson, but was still guiding him (15:14-15)?

In chapter 16 what do we learn was Samson's weakness?

Why did Samson reveal his secret?

What happened to Samson's fellowship with God (16:20-21)?

Samson was made a slave, or a work animal, for he was tied between two millstones and relegated to grinding meal. Judges 16:22 makes me think of the chorus "God Is so Good."

Patsy Campbell

How does God show goodness to Samson (16:22)?

_____

_____

How does God give Samson the victory?

_____

_____

_____

In getting the victory, what happens to Samson (16:30)?

_____

_____

It *is* truly all about You, Lord. Only You have the power of life and death. Samson got the victory over the Philistines, but in getting it God took his life. Disobedience is so costly; but God promised victory, and Samson wisely claimed the promise.

The third example from our list is found in John 18:15-27.

Who is the main character in this passage? _____

What does *deny* mean?

_____

_____

Why is denial so serious for the child of God? _____

_____

_____

_____

How many times did Peter deny Jesus? _____

What caused Peter to be reminded of his denials (18:27)?

_____

Pray, Work, Win!

Do you ever hear the cock crow in your own life? Explain.

_____

_____

_____

Peter's life shows us that our actions make an impression, but so do our reactions. Peter reacted to the maid's question with denial, and he reacted to the officers at the fire with denial. Three denials, then a common sound in those days became the voice of Peter's conscience. Yes, the cock did crow. But let's remember, it's all about You, Lord. God still loved Peter. God still had work for Peter. Peter stood at the door outside. He was cozy with the enemy and used their fire to warm himself. Later, Peter tells the Lord three times, *"Thou knowest ... I love thee"* (John 21:15-17). Don't you know this was humiliating to Peter for his Lord to ask the same question three times, *"Lovest thou me?"* The Lord was taking away any pride. Deny three times; affirm three times. The Lord tells Peter to feed His sheep. How can Peter do this? Do you remember Pentecost? Peter denied three times. Peter affirmed his love three times. On the day of Pentecost God took that three, added three zeroes, and gave Peter the victory as three thousand souls were saved and added to the church. Acts 2:41 is the reference for this victory.

Peter went from being by the fire of the enemy to being *on fire for God*. Peter had a burning passion to preach the Word and see souls saved. Only You, Lord, can transform a mere man in such a way. Let us each get a vision that what the Lord did for Peter, He will do for each one of us who wants the victory. Yes, it's all about You, Lord.

The last example on our list is from Joshua 5:13-6:27. I want you to do a mini study of your own. Make up your own questions. Write the answers. At the end do a summation showing "It's all about You, Lord."

Your study is "Will the Wall Fall?" based on the scriptures listed above in Joshua. This is a great study and I want you to know I am not just being lazy. This exercise will help you experience some growth in your Bible study. Be sure to examine in detail how the battle plan shows "It's all about You, Lord." Only God could have planned that battle. Use the following space to outline your study.

_____

_____

_____

_____

I hope that completing these four mini studies has brought a deeper meaning in your life to the phrase "It's all about You, Lord." I love the portion of Exodus 34:6 which says, *"The LORD, The LORD God, merciful and gracious, longsuffering, and abundant in goodness and truth."* The Lord, Yahweh, is self-existent. There never was a time when He was not. He is Who He is. It's all about You, Lord.

Pray, Work, Win!

Chapter 11

Never Give Up

Salvation, commitment, and perseverance are all important in our praying, our working, and our winning. The perseverance is a *must* if we are to be winners. We will fail. We will give up. We will need restoration. So we must persevere. Every day we need to be at work for God. Persevere in the following work from God's Word.

Write 1 Corinthians 15:58 here.

_____
_____
_____
_____
_____

Define *steadfast*.

_____
_____

Define *unmovable*.

_____
_____

Define *abounding*.

_____
_____

What will happen to our labor for the Lord?

_____
_____

Pray, Work, Win!

Write 1 Corinthians 16:13-14 here. How do these two verses relate to our perseverance? How do they relate to maturity?

_____
_____
_____
_____
_____
_____
_____
_____

Write Ephesians 6:18 here.

_____
_____
_____

Why is prayer required for us to be able to persevere?

_____
_____
_____
_____

Write 2 Thessalonians 3:13 here.

_____
_____
_____

How does this verse teach that the Lord knows us really well? _____

_____
_____
_____

Patsy Campbell

Write Hebrews 10:23, 38 here.

_____
_____
_____
_____
_____
_____

It is a good idea to relive our salvation experience often in order to be able to persevere. Why?

_____
_____
_____
_____

Write 2 Peter 3:17-18 here.

_____
_____
_____
_____
_____
_____
_____

How does perseverance help us grow in grace and knowledge?

_____
_____
_____
_____

Pray, Work, Win!

How will our perseverance cause us to give all the glory to God and want none for ourselves?

_____

_____

Write Revelation 2:25-27 here.

_____

_____

_____

_____

_____

_____

How long shall we hold fast?

_____

What reward(s) do these verses teach that faithful believers will earn?

_____

I would like to end this section by telling you about a victory the Lord has allowed our church to enjoy for ten years. I am sharing this because it amplifies the concepts of pray, work, win — the three sections of this book.

Several members on a planning committee read the book *Don't Just Stand There, Pray Something* by Ronald Dunn. These members began to pray for God to show His plan for a prayer ministry in our church. Remember back in section 2 we studied a topic on organization and making a plan with orderly steps. Well, a coordinator was chosen for what was called Park Place Intercessory Prayer Ministry.

The group chose the first Saturday of each month from 6:00 a.m. to 6:00 p.m. as the time for this special ministry. They recruited twelve prayer teams of two members each. Each team took a one-hour shift on these days. These teams have changed very little over the years, and we have several very faithful substitutes to fill any gaps. As we have persevered, God has been very faithful to provide the needed people.

Patsy Campbell

    We set aside a room as a prayer room and furnished it for this purpose. We still use the same room and a prayer team also uses it each Sunday morning to pray for all phases of the morning worship service. Our mission prayer group meets in this room every Sunday morning before Sunday School. As you can see, this room gets used frequently.

    We developed the necessary forms for the prayer ministry. The coordinator purchased a Rolodex file with cards and updates it each month. Each team member receives a reminder letter each month, and the entire church membership is encouraged to write request forms to be placed in the file. This ministry takes constant working to make it successful.

    I am writing this section of the book at the church building, and it is prayer day. As I look at the clock, the sixth-hour team is now praying. For ten years God has given us the victory with so many answered prayers, souls saved, and lives strengthened. What a blessing this ministry has been. God has been faithful to us in this ministry because Park Place has persevered, been committed, and remained faithful to God. As we pray, God works and answers. Praise be to God!

    The top rung of salvation, prayer, work, and winning is a great place to be. We are feeling great about our deep fellowship with our heavenly Father and tasting the victories only God can give. I hope it feels like holy ground to you. Let's walk on it every day.

Epilogue — Pray, Work, Win

Who exemplifies this attitude in God's book? Many come to mind, but I want to end with a short study on Nehemiah. He really used prayer, planned, and did his work daily and faithfully. God, the great rewarder, gave Nehemiah a great victory. The ruins became reality. A wall stood completed in such a short time.

Was Nehemiah a priest or a layman? _____
This has great significance for us. Tell why.

_____
_____
_____

Nehemiah 1 tells us in the first few verses what Nehemiah learned about Jerusalem and the walls.
What did Nehemiah do (1:4)?

1. _____
2. _____
3. _____
4. _____
5. _____

What is the significance of each action?

1. _____
2. _____
3. _____
4. _____
5. _____

Why did Nehemiah pray for King Artaxerxes?

_____
_____
_____

Pray, Work, Win!

What happens in Nehemiah 2 that shows God heard and answered Nehemiah's prayers?

_____
_____
_____
_____
_____

What was the first thing Nehemiah did when he arrived at Jerusalem (2:9-16)?

_____
_____
_____

What was the second thing he did (2:17-20)?

_____
_____
_____

Nehemiah 3 is the salvation story in the gates of Jerusalem. It would make a wonderful study for your quiet time. It will truly bless your heart.

Nehemiah 4-6 shows that Satan is really busy. He sends opposition. Discuss the three types of opposition faced by Nehemiah and his people.

1. _____
_____
_____

2. _____
_____
_____

3. _____
_____
_____

Patsy Campbell

Leaders have to be good role models and set an example. How did Nehemiah set a good example in Nehemiah 5:14-19?

_____

_____
_____
_____
_____
_____

How long did it take to build the wall (6:15)? _____
Do you think the people were surprised at how quickly it happened?

_____

What do you think Nehemiah thought and felt?

_____
_____
_____
_____

How was all this work possible?

_____
_____
_____

Remember, God can do anything, absolutely anything. That is why we call Him God. Nehemiah prayed, planned, encouraged, enlisted, and worked. Then God gave the victory. Nehemiah shows us the people were given so much more than just a finished wall.

What does Nehemiah 8 teach?

_____
_____
_____
_____

Pray, Work, Win!

The people fasted and repented. They were personally preparing themselves to enjoy the victory of God.

What happened in Nehemiah 10?

_____

_____

_____

_____

_____

_____

Nehemiah 12 records the dedication of the wall. Victory brings joy and praise. What happened at the dedication (12:27)?

1. _____
2. _____
3. _____
4. _____
5. _____
6. _____

What else happened (12:43)?

_____

_____

_____

_____

The temple was cleaned and its procedures were reinstated. The book of Moses was read. The enemies who caused opposition were repudiated. The priests received provision, and the rest of the Sabbath was put in place again. Praise the Lord for He gives us so much more than we could ever envision.

Pray, Work, Win

Nehemiah prayed about everything and so should we. He asked God to show him the work God wanted. Nehemiah observed, planned, and waited on God to say, "It is time." So should we. Nehemiah enjoyed the victory that only God could give. So can we.

Patsy Campbell

Moses encouraged the people in Exodus 14:13-14 to (1) fear not, (2) stand still, and (3) see that *"The LORD shall fight for you, and ye shall hold your peace"* (verse 14).

Don't you want this to happen in your life? *Pray* and have a quiet time everyday. Find God's *work* that He has called you to do — not everything, but just your work. Trust and believe you will *win*. Victory after victory will be yours to claim because God loves you and wants you to succeed.

Please begin now to *pray*, *work*, and *win*. God bless you on this journey of a lifetime.

Pray, Work, Win!